be happy

OTHER BOOKS, AUDIO BOOKS, AND DVDS BY HANK SMITH

Mothers Are Like . . .

Thou Shalt Be Nice

Real Life

Be Who You Are

My Soul Hungered

Break Up with the World

Do's and Don'ts of Dating

I Love My Friends

5 Temptation Killers

Running Down Your Dreams

Scripture Power

Wake Up from Your Phone

Being Happy in an Unhappy World

Fighting For Not with Your Family

Unshaken

Build Your House upon a Rock

Be of Good Cheer

Unconquerable

Hank Smith Live (DVD)

Laugh and Learn (DVD)

be happy

Simple Secrets to a Happier Life

Hank Smith, PhD

Covenant Communications, Inc.

Published by Covenant Communications, Inc.
American Fork, Utah

Printed in the United States of America
First Printing: February 2017

23 22 21 20 19 18 17 10 9 8 7 6 5 4 3 2 1

ISBN 978-1-52440-263-1

To Sara and my five favorite kiddos on the planet.
I love you. To me, you are happiness.

To my editor, Kathy Gordon—you are incredible!
Your gifts brought this book to light.

TABLE OF CONTENTS

INTRODUCTION

Happiness.

We all want it. We all seek it . . . Every. Single. Day.

We all want to be the person who friends and family describe as full of light and happiness. The one about whom others say, "I love being around you. You are so uplifting!"

What's the big deal? And exactly what *is* happiness, anyway?

Sometimes it's easier to go in the back door—to define what happiness is *not.*

I have a perfect example, and you'll get what I mean right off the bat.

One night one of my friends had to take her four-year-old granddaughter to the emergency room: my friend was babysitting, and Brooklyn had spiked one of those fevers that you're convinced means certain death. As they rolled into the parking lot, Brooklyn was curled up in a fierce ball, practically shrink-wrapped in her favorite blankie.

"I don't want to go in there, Granny," she whimpered. "They're going to give me a shot."

Granny, hoping Brooklyn would man up and go in voluntarily, soothingly responded, "Oh, honey, I don't think they'll give you a shot. They just need to figure out what made you sick so they can help you."

Brief pause in the programming to mention that you should never make promises to a kid that you can't keep. But that will have to wait for next time.

Back to the ER parking lot: After ten more minutes of pleading and cajoling—and Granny's increasingly intense promises of no shots—Brooklyn finally decided to throw her fate to the wind. Whisked off to an examining room, she lay atop a table while four nurses towered over her, attempting to start an IV. And you know what that means: a NEEDLE.

Ever seen someone try to start an IV on a four-year-old? You know—a kid with veins the size of fishing line? I'll spare you the lurid details and just say there was a lot of poking and prodding going on. And if looks could kill, the ones coming from Brooklyn would have made Granny a grease spot on the floor.

Finally, the eagle landed. As the nurses taped down the tubing and gathered up their supplies, Brooklyn sat up, squared up her shoulders, and in a voice that thundered all the way to the south end of the county boldly proclaimed, "I. AM. NOT. HAPPY!"

There you have it—a stellar example of what happiness is NOT. Take it from Brooklyn, because she knows.

Now that we know what happiness is not, let's return to the original question: What *is* happiness, and why is it so naturally important to us? Everyone occasionally experiences unhappiness, and I think I can go out on a strong limb here and say that everyone wants to be happier. The desire to be happy is ingrained in you. The Lord put it there. You might think of it as His fingerprint on your brain. In these pages, you will learn what happiness is, where it comes from, what its barriers are, and how you can get more of it.

Because we desire happiness so much, we might think of unhappiness as the enemy, something to be defeated entirely, but that isn't the case at all. Unhappiness can be an excellent teacher. Occasional bouts with difficult circumstances and unhappiness often humble us and disrupt bad habits. President Boyd K. Packer once said, "It was meant to be that life would be a challenge. To suffer some anxiety, some depression, some disappointment, even some failure is normal." President Packer was telling us that the world is a classroom designed to give you problems. Wait. On purpose? Yep.

Good times.

But wait—that's not all. Check out what President Packer said next: "If you have a good miserable day once in a while, or several in a row, stand steady and face them. Things will straighten out. *There's great purpose in our struggle in life.*"

That's right: there *is* great purpose in life, even in the hard parts, and I will tell you without any reservation that even through the hard parts, you can experience happiness. In fact, happiness is one of the most important conditions you can achieve in this life. Even—and maybe especially—while you're *also* having problems. Happiness does not mean being free from problems and trials, but finding purpose in problems and trials can result in abundant happiness.

I can hear what you're thinking right now: *Well, that's easy for* him *to say. He doesn't have to deal with* my *problems.* And you're right. I *don't* have to deal with your problems. I don't even know what they are. But I've met countless people with significant trials—stuff you'd never imagine—and I've found that no matter how many problems creep in, many of them truthfully describe their lives as happy and very happy. This book can help you join the happy crowd.

> I've met countless people who have significant trials, and many of them truthfully describe their lives as very happy.

For example, I'd like to introduce you to two of my friends, Richie and Natalie Norton. They're sort of the movers and shakers of the thirty-somethings in the Church.

He's an author, sought-after speaker, social entrepreneur, CEO, consultant for the corporate growth and personal development industries, and expert in self-reliance. He was recognized by *Pacific Business News* as one of the "top forty under 40 best and brightest young businessmen in Hawaii." He was also published in the *Journal of Microfinance* and was an awardwinner for outstanding accomplishment in international development, international relations, humanitarian aid, and academic achievement.

Ready to come up for air yet?

Richie's wife, Natalie, is no slouch either. She's a popular blogger, celebrity wedding and portrait photographer, popular speaker, and educator in entrepreneurship and peak performance. She has recently developed a workshop that empowers moms with the tools they need to achieve success in entrepreneurial efforts while maintaining balance and harmony at home. And her work has been published in *Exquisite Bride*, *InStyle Weddings*, and *Ceremony Magazine*.

So you're probably thinking that Richie and Natalie have nothing to complain about. Oh, how wrong you are. Talk about trials. It hurts my heart to even think about it. These two have a PhD in problems with a specialty in loss. In fact, the loss they've endured almost boggles the mind.

Here's just one example of what I'm talking about. Five years ago, they welcomed their fourth baby boy—Gavin David Bruce Norton, named after Natalie's only sibling, who died at the age of twenty-one (Gavin had lived with Richie and Natalie for many years before passing away). Though they had completely welcomed each of their children, there was something a bit different with Gavin; as Natalie tells it, "We just felt absolute joy—just elation."

When Gavin was two months old, he received a clean bill of health from his pediatrician in Hawaii and a green light to fly to Utah, where his parents would visit family. A week later, Gavin developed a cough. After an initial diagnosis of RSV, Gavin rapidly deteriorated. His concerned parents rushed him to the emergency room at Primary Children's Hospital. There, eight-week-old Gavin was diagnosed with pertussis—whooping cough—and began a ferocious fight for his life. He lost that fight two weeks later as he quietly slipped through the veil.

Richie remembers the experience as "horrifying." Natalie describes the terror of standing there watching her child die and not being able to do anything about it. Yet they also remember the moment they knew "the heavens opened," a small blip on the radar of time when they felt pure love for their baby boy and his life. "We snuggled him and we sang to him," Natalie remembers, "and we said good-bye."

Gavin was buried next to the uncle for whom he was named.

This is just one example of the kinds of loss this couple has endured. Yet they are some of the happiest people I know. Anyone who knows them can see it. In one of his blogs, Richie talked about their commitment to having fun—to being happy no matter what. They do stuff like blast the radio to fun songs in the car. Hold impromptu dance parties in the grocery store. Play the guitar and scream loud enough to wake the babies next door. Watch movies with the kids on Friday nights, complete with enough treats to sink the *Titanic.*

They are happy after such a tragedy? Yes. Absolutely, yes. Natalie believes with all her heart that "Gavin's purpose was to help people know that they have a Father in Heaven who loves them."

Their perspective on their trials is important in allowing Richie and Natalie to be happy despite a litany of loss that, were it not for their attitude, could have put them under. Natalie once told me, "I've come to realize that this life is an experience of loss—that we've come here to learn how to deal with loss. I no longer fear loss like I used to because I realize that it's part of our purpose in life. Life is almost designed that way."

Sound like something you read just a minute ago? Yep. Sounds just like President Packer, doesn't it? And you *know* what they say about being in the mouth of two witnesses . . . (and it sure doesn't hurt that one is a mom and the other an Apostle, which is almost as good as a mom).

Let's start simple. Here's a key to understanding happiness: There are two kinds of happiness—the kind that happens *to* you and the kind that happens *inside of* you—and you can be truly happy only if you have the second kind of happiness.

Most people get that confused. They think that *real* happiness comes from the first kind—the kind that results when something awesome happens to you. You know: You get a new car with all the bells and whistles. You get a raise. You get a kitchen remodel. You go to Disneyland. You get the very best present under the Christmas tree. You find out you don't need a root canal after all.

Sure—all those things are pretty much guaranteed to put a smile on your face. And lots of people mistake that for *happiness.* But despite that big cheesy smile on your face, that happiness won't last. Because, you see, those things are temporary—what we call *transitory.*

You could get in a wreck in your new car. You might find out that your new raise shoves you into the next tax bracket, resulting in a net loss. And the root canal might be on the docket in a few months after all. That kind of happiness is based on circumstances that are often outside of your control.

Real happiness—the genuine, lasting kind of happiness—comes from within. It's part of who you are. It doesn't depend on what happens to you. It survives the fender benders and the increased tax bills and the root canals and all the other storms of life.

Real happiness—the genuine, lasting kind of happiness—comes from within. It's part of who you are. It doesn't depend on what happens to you.

I once heard a little story that illustrates the genuine kind of happiness for which we should all strive. I've never forgotten it, and I'd like to share it here.

A woman who was traveling in the mountains stopped at a stream and was resting there when she saw through the waters what looked like a precious stone settled in the sands of the streambed. Plucking the stone carefully out of the meandering waters, she turned it over and over, examining it in the sunlight, and immediately recognized that it was a stone of astonishing value. Grateful for her good luck in finding the stone, she tucked it inside her bag and continued her journey.

The next day, the woman met another traveler who said he was desperately hungry. When the woman opened her bag to share her food, the hungry traveler saw the precious stone. Forgetting all about his physical hunger, he asked the woman to give him the stone.

She did so without hesitation.

The traveler practically sprinted off down the path, rejoicing in his good fortune. He knew that the stone was worth enough to provide him security for a lifetime. As for the woman, she happily continued on her journey, not diminished a single bit by the fact that she no longer had the stone.

A few days later, she was surprised to yet again meet the same traveler on her path. She was even more surprised when he held out his hand to her, the precious stone cradled in his palm.

"I've been thinking," he said, meeting her eyes. "I know how valuable this stone is. But I'll give it back to you in the hope that you can give me something even more precious."

"What is it you seek?" asked the woman.

"Please give me what you have within you that enabled you to give me the stone without any reluctance," he responded. "How did you do that?"

I hope you suspect by now that the woman was able to hand over the stone—a priceless treasure—because finding that stone was *not* what made her happy. Her happiness came from within. It was there with or without the stone. And it was going to last forever.

It's the kind of happiness Richie and Natalie Norton have. It's a happiness that lasts forever and that enriches their lives, even while enduring countless storms. Even after having their beautiful ten-week-old son pass away in their arms.

And here's the best part: *You can have that kind of happiness.* You can be happy—solidly, genuinely happy—no matter what's going on around you, no matter what happens *to* you, no matter what storm comes along to batter and bruise you.

Keep reading, and I'll show you how.

CHAPTER ONE
The Science of Happiness

Scientists know a lot about happiness, and I'd like to share their research with you because it will help you understand how happiness originates. The Lord encourages us to seek truth wherever we can find it, right? Well, brilliant researchers definitely have some truth about happiness that can teach us valuable lessons. Don't panic. Nothing I tell you here is going to be so complicated that you need a PhD to unravel it. (Honestly, though, I got a PhD, which means anyone can do it.) I've left all of that stuff to my scholarly friends (they don't like to associate with me in public anyway), and I'm going to give you the *Reader's Digest* condensed, simplified version. You're going to love it.

Maybe you have as much happiness as you can possibly handle. If so, congratulations! Even so, humor me. Keep reading. Because you're going to learn a lot about happiness in the pages that follow—stuff that will help you understand yourself better, and even more stuff that will help you understand the people you love. You might even learn some things that could make you positively delirious with happiness—and who wouldn't want *that*?

I'm willing to bet, though, based on sheer statistics, that maybe you feel you could be a little happier. Let's take a look at those statistics, because they're fascinating.

Let's start with the most important. Remember these numbers. Here's what the world's best researchers have found about the sources of happiness: Genetic tendencies (that's right—good old DNA) are 50 percent responsible for happiness. Intentional activities—the things I'll teach you how to do—are 40 percent responsible for happiness. And that leaves only a whopping *10 percent*. You read that right: your circumstances are responsible for *only 10 percent of your happiness.*

Circumstances and Happiness

The National Opinion Research Center does a general survey every decade that measures the happiness of Americans. In 1980, only 35 percent of those surveyed said they were "very happy." Another 12 percent said they were "not too happy." The rest fell somewhere in between.

Here's what fascinates me: those percentages stayed roughly the same over the next thirty years.

Then, in 2010, check out what the survey revealed: 14 percent were "not too happy." Only 29 percent felt "very happy." These aren't the kinds of statistical differences that make headline news, but they're important: they definitely show that fewer people are very happy and more people are not all that happy than was the case thirty years ago.

I'm just going to come right out and say that this could seem strange on the surface. In the last thirty-plus years, a *lot* has changed. We have faster, more luxurious cars. Our cell phones have more processing power than the ship that landed on the moon! We have microwaves that do it all at the touch of a button (we'll talk more about microwaves and happiness later). We have computers that in seconds can do the work that used to take hours or days. We have dishwashers that conquer baked-on lasagna. We can watch our favorite TV programs on our phones, our notepads, or our laptops—no more being chained to the television set. We have watches that will monitor our heart rate, tell us how much oxygen we're getting, and keep track of every step we take. We can go shopping online and, with the mere click of a button, have practically anything we want delivered right to our doorstep in a day or two. We can record any TV show we want and watch it whenever

> Your circumstances are responsible for only 10 percent of your happiness.

we want, zipping through all those annoying commercials. There is no doubt that we have cooler stuff than any human beings have ever had in the history of the world.

And that means that we should be happier. Right?

Nope.

But why? After all, the commercials on television—*if* you watch them—communicate a subtle but powerful message: *Stuff equals happiness. The more stuff you have, the happier you'll be.*

And it's not just TV. Think about the billboards you see as you drive down the road. *You need this. You need that. If you don't look like this, you need to fix it right away, and do we have the answer for you! And here's a problem you didn't even* know *you had—but we can solve it!* Nothing like creating a problem and a solution in the 4.3 seconds it takes you to sail past the sign!

But science doesn't back up the billboards or the television commercials. Here are the facts of life on happiness: that car, that smartphone, that microwave, that notebook computer, not even that online shopping site will make you happier.

What? The new car, the trip to Disneyland, the fancy new microwave, the online shopping spree has only a negligible impact on happiness? That's right. Each of those things can result in *pleasure*, or maybe a temporary high—but none results in lasting happiness. Happiness is something much deeper, much more lasting. Bigger and even more amazing than Disneyland.

You might be fighting this notion right now. You might be thinking, *That's got to be wrong. I* know *my circumstances have a* lot *to do with how happy I am*. I used to think the same thing, but it's simply not true. This isn't just an important religious principle; it is backed up by solid scientific research.

Let's start with a famous study done in 1978. This was real, well-designed research, not an online CNN quick poll. In this study, scientists compared two groups of people—those who had just won the lottery and those who had just become paraplegics—and measured their happiness levels.

Quick time-out. If you were asked who might be happier, a person who just won the lottery or a person who just found out they would never be able to use their legs again, which would you say?

This isn't a trick question. You'd probably say the lucky soul rolling in the dough would be *much* happier than the unfortunate person who is now going to live in a wheelchair forever.

Well, you would be wrong. So were the scientists who thought that same logical thing before they did the study. But here's what they found based on hard evidence: the lottery winners and the paraplegics had the exact same happiness levels one year after their defining event. There was a temporary uptick in happiness for the lottery winners and a temporary decline in happiness for the paraplegics, but after a year the paraplegics were just as happy as the lottery winners. It's this little thing called *hedonic adaptation*, which simply means conditions that once made you exhilaratingly happy just don't do it for you after a while, and things that once made you horribly sad don't seem like much of a problem anymore. See, I told you—*circumstances don't define happiness.*

> **Your brain adapts. Things that once made you exhilaratingly happy just don't do it for you after a while.**

People who believe all their happiness depends on circumstances fall into a dangerous trap. They think that happiness will be in the next place, with the next job, with the next partner, and so on. You'll chase it your entire life and never catch it because it wasn't ever there in the first place. And until you give up on the idea that happiness is somewhere else, it will *never* be where you are.

This truth is one of the most difficult to accept. I couldn't accept it even after reading all the research. I used to think: *This is wrong. Circumstances are* everything *when it comes to happiness! If I were just thinner-younger-richer-smarter-healthier, I would* for sure *be happier!*

The research would always respond: *No. No, you wouldn't. Not in the deep, quenching, real, satisfying way.*

Oh, you might have a few fleeting moments of pleasure, but that's not happiness. Those are two very different things. Something that brings you pleasure triggers the reward center in your brain, and boy, does it love you. And you love it, even though you're not consciously aware of it. There's nothing wrong with pleasure when it comes from a pure source (and we're not even going to *touch* on all the impure ways you can get pleasure!). It's just that pleasure is temporary. It's fleeting. It's the trip to Disneyland, the new couch, the new car. Sooner rather than later, the thrill of those things wears off.

Real happiness never wears off. It's there through the ups and downs, and it brings with it the joy that keeps you going. Joseph Smith knew about it almost two hundred years ago. The Savior knew all about it more than two thousand years ago. If you want to get some real insight into happiness, study what both of them had to say about how we should live our lives. Chapter 3 will get you started.

Here's what happens with the pleasure that comes from circumstances: the new car, the new house, the new furniture, the new cell phone, the new whatever it was you just *had* to have might actually make you happy . . . for a minute. (Okay, maybe more than a *minute*, but not much more.) Martin E. P. Seligman, the father of positive psychology and one of the most respected psychologists of our time, compares this phenomenon to ice cream or pizza. The first bite is THE BEST. Oh, man, it's good. The second bite is still pretty great, but not *quite* as good as the first bite. The third bite is okay, but now it's going downhill a little. By the ninth or tenth bite, you want something else. In other words, you need a different "high."

That's how it is with circumstances . . . with "stuff." The first time you drive that new car, it's amazing. You can't believe how great it is. Come on, this *has* to be the epitome of happiness. But hang on—two weeks later, you're not feeling that same buzz every time you climb in and back out of the driveway. A month later, it's old hat. Now you're looking for something else to give you a buzz. Do you remember the name of this unpleasant phenomenon? That right, hedonic adaptation.

I have to take a quick time out to give an important disclaimer. When it comes to circumstances, there are two exceptions to what

I've been saying—two circumstances that can significantly impact your happiness. One is serious, chronic illness, the kind that disables you to a point that you are unable to do the things that are important to you. The other is poverty—and I mean real destitution, where you're living below the poverty line and can't meet your family's basic needs. These two things are the circumstances that impact your happiness. Dress size and shopping sprees and vacations are *not.*

DNA and Happiness

If happiness is only slightly contingent upon circumstances, where does it originate?

You may have first thought of *the heart.* You've probably heard it said that the heart is the center of all emotion. You could probably name many songs and speeches about the power of the heart to love and lead and conquer all.

Well, not really. The heart is an amazing organ made up of muscle and chambers and valves that pumps oxygen-rich blood throughout your body. It's critical to life. Without the heart, you'd die. But it doesn't have anything to do with happiness, or any other emotion. Sorry to burst that little bubble.

No, ladies and gentlemen, happiness originates in your mind—that little gray, squiggly, three-and-a-half-pound mass of nerves and tissue that sits inside your skull. The brain just isn't as romantic as the heart. (Maybe Valentine's Day should be filled with pictures of little brains and candies shaped like brains and lovers exclaiming, "I love you with all of my brain!") The brain matters to happiness, and not just a little. Remember that I told you that 50 percent, fully *half,* of your happiness comes from your DNA? It does. It's been well researched. So if you're generally a very happy person, you can thank your parents. If, on the other hand, you're generally pretty miserable, you can settle into the therapist's couch and blame your parents.

The human mind is enormously complex, even mysterious, but because of technological advances, neurological researchers know much more about the brain than they did just one or two decades ago. For thousands of years of medical practice no one could examine a brain unless the person attached to it was dead. That had to be frustrating. That's like trying to analyze and program a computer without a power cord. You can look at it, but it is incredibly difficult to determine what's working correctly and what's not.

Well, thanks to neuroimaging, we can now examine the human brain while its owner is still very much alive. We can watch the brain in action, real time. We can see how all kinds of things affect it. And we can see which parts are responsible for which things. There is still much to be discovered in neuroscience, but the last few decades have brought valuable insight about the brain to light. Each year we learn more and more. It is fascinating and exciting.

As humans, we have three basic lobes in the brain. The one that sits in front, directly behind your forehead, is the *frontal lobe*. It's what separates you from the animals.

Here's how. A dog gets hungry. He eats. That's it, he has no frontal lobe to analyze his behavior. Now look what we humans do. We get hungry. We decide to eat. But, oh no—it's never that simple. The brain kicks into gear and asks, *Why am I eating? Should I really eat* that*? It has too many calories. I should find something with fewer carbs. Oh, wait—I shouldn't eat right now. I should wait until dinner. This is going to ruin my appetite. Maybe I'm not really hungry.* Congratulations, you've just met your frontal lobe, the part of your brain that makes you different from the animals. The frontal lobe allows you to think about your thoughts and analyze your behavior. As far as we know, no other creature on the planet can do that. The frontal lobe is the great separator.

The frontal lobe of your brain allows you to think about your thoughts and analyze your behavior. As far as we know, no other creature on the planet can do that.

And something else is happening in the frontal lobe: happiness.

Here's what happens. Your brain is made up of billions of little neurons. They're like teeny tiny cell phones. There are spaces between these neurons called *synapses*. And there are substances called *neurotransmitters* that bridge those spaces and allow the neurons to send messages to each other—neurotransmitters function kind of like WiFi signals in your brain. What you have is sort of like billions of people sending texts to each other on those billions of tiny cell phones. And it all happens with lightning speed. I don't know what version of iPhone you have, but your brain is an iPhone 500.

The neurotransmitters—the microscopic WiFi signals in your brain—have to be working if the neurons are going to communicate with each other. They carry the message. If there's no message, nothing happens. It's like your cell phone has no bars—no service. Suddenly there are billions of teeny little cell phones and many of them can't communicate with each other. That freaks them out. Hello, anxiety!

And here's what those neurons are saying in your brain: *I should be feeling happy right now.* Nothing. *Hold everything—I should be feeling good right now.* Nope. Nothing. *Where's the message? What's going on? I'm not getting the message! Where's the message? Something's wrong!* And then you can guess what happens: the brain goes into panic mode. And the next thing you know, you are panicking *over nothing.* You feel like something horrible is about to happen all the time, and you don't know why. All of a sudden, the neurons are getting the message, all right, but it's not the message they wanted or anticipated: *Something is wrong. Something is terribly wrong.* Uh-oh—now you have a panic attack. And this sort of thing might go on for months.

If you've never had a panic attack, think of the most terrifying experience you've ever had and you'll have an idea of what it is like. Someone having a panic attack is, as the name implies, gripped with panic—usually without even knowing why. She's trying to stay calm. She's mentally repeating, *I'm okay. I'm okay.* Except she isn't. It really feels like she's under attack. She feels like she might fall off that cliff, but there is no cliff in sight. She loses control. Her heart starts racing and pounding; she starts sweating profusely. She can't breathe; she might feel like she is choking or being smothered. She feels dizzy, light-headed, or faint and may develop numbness or tingling sensations in her arms and legs. She may have such intense chest pain that she fears she is having a heart attack. Possibly worst of all, she feels detached from herself or that things suddenly aren't real; many victims of panic attacks are convinced they are dying.

She may have been driving down the freeway to get her kids to soccer camp. Suddenly, she has to veer onto the shoulder of the road and lie across the seat, even though she doesn't want to. She's gasping for air. From the backseat comes a small, scared voice: "Mom, what's wrong?"

Let me be perfectly clear here. She didn't *want* to pull off the freeway. She didn't *want* to lay across the seats. She *wanted* to take her kids to soccer camp. A lot of those little cell phones in her brain are panicking. And when that happens, there are serious repercussions.

Forty years ago, a person who acted like that got all kinds of harsh responses, both from themselves and others. "Snap out of it." "You're so spoiled; grow up!" "Stop acting like a child throwing a tantrum." "You know what your problem is? You don't go to the temple often enough." "If you only had more faith." Fast-forward forty years, and we have the ability to watch how the brain is working, live and in real time. We can *see* what's happening to cause a panic attack. And it's not being spoiled or throwing a tantrum or slacking off on temple attendance. It's none of those things. It's a disruption of the neurotransmitters in the brain. The signals are shutting down. Depression and anxiety are not character problems, they are chemistry problems.

DNA determines the level of those neurotransmitters—the chemicals that allow all the communication to take place. Your DNA determines the amount of neurotransmitters (they have fun names like dopamine, serotonin, and norepinephrine) in your brain, and neurotransmitters make sure that all those neurons are communicating like they should be.

Have you ever known someone who was just naturally happy? You know, the kind of person who drives down the street with a big smile on his face? The kind of person who loves everyone and everything? You can be pretty sure that the perpetually happy soul got dealt a good hand of cards in the DNA game.

So what if you happened to get a really bad hand of cards in the DNA game? Does that mean you're dead in the water—that you'll never be happy and there's nothing you can do about it? Absolutely not. First of all, we're talking just *half*—there's another half that you can pretty much control, and you'll learn how in this book. And that's not all. If the chemicals in your brain are just not working the way they're supposed to because of inherited tendencies (aka depression, anxiety, etc.), there are medications and practices that can get those chemicals to healthy levels. Your doctor can help. Here's one thing we know for sure: don't just ignore it, because it *won't* go away. More about that in chapter 6.

Intentional Happiness

Now let's move on to the thing that's responsible for 40 percent of your happiness: intentional activities. In other words, 40 percent of your happiness comes from the things you do to manage your happiness—your behavior. Dr. Seligman calls it passion; he says that the happiest people are those who have found their specific gifts and who use those gifts in a cause greater than themselves. He calls it getting into the flow. And getting into the flow brings great happiness that lasts far longer than the scent of the leather seats in your new car.

> Forty percent of your happiness comes from the things you do to manage your happiness—your behavior.

To illustrate, let's look at a woman we'll call Melissa. Melissa was in college, and she was working part-time bagging groceries to help support herself. But Melissa had a big problem: she *hated* her job. She was absolutely miserable. Every day as she put on her dopey little apron and marched through the doors of that blasted grocery store, she thought, *I'd rather be having a spinal tap than putting another head of cauliflower in a grocery bag.* But times were tough, and part-time jobs weren't exactly plentiful, and she really needed the cash, so she was basically stuck.

Then something wonderful happened. Melissa gradually recognized one of her gifts: she realized that she was a real "people person." And it occurred to her that she could be using that gift in her job. Melissa made a conscious decision to break out of her shell and actually *talk* to every person who came through the line. At first it was difficult, but it became easier and easier. And suddenly she saw her job in a whole new way: it wasn't about bags of groceries or heads of cauliflower but about people. *She had the ability to make a person's day.*

With all of that came a remarkable thing: Melissa became *happier*. She got into the flow. Instead of dreading her work every day, she loved what she was doing. Time flew. Every day when she clocked out, she found she couldn't wait to come back the next day. And you can bet that her happiness spilled over into every aspect of her life.

Identifying and using your gifts is a major key to happiness. And your happiness becomes even greater when you not only use your gifts on a daily basis, but when you use your gifts to forward a cause you see as more important than your own happiness—to achieve a higher purpose. Evangelical Christian pastor Rick Warren advanced this idea in his book, *The Purpose-Driven Life: What on Earth Am I Here For?* In order to achieve lasting, quenching happiness, we each need to ask and answer that question: *What on earth am I here for?* Warren counseled, "Experience is not what happens to you. It is what you do with what happens to you. Don't waste your pain; use it to help others."

In his book, Warren writes, "The only really happy people are those who have learned how to serve." Sound familiar? The Lord already knew this, so He gave us a church in which we are able to serve. That means everyone from the nursery workers to the bishop. Maybe you feel that one of your major purposes in life is to forward the Lord's work in the kingdom of God. The Lord designed it that way, and He gave you gifts so you could do just that. In the scriptures, He calls them spiritual gifts—talents. And if you've identified that as a way to fulfill your purpose, congratulations—you've found it. It's almost as if the Lord knew about happiness before scientists did!

For just a second, contrast that purpose-driven life with what we'd call a pleasure-driven life. Instead of drenching yourself in something bigger than yourself, working to achieve a higher purpose, you're on a crash course to grab all the pleasure you can from wherever you can, always looking around the next corner for something to make you "happy." King Benjamin called this guy the "natural man." Warren put it about as plainly as you can: "You cannot fulfil God's purposes for your life while focusing on your own plans." In other words, forget the "things." Get past the "stuff."

You cannot fulfil God's purposes for your life while focusing on your own plans.

By now, you should understand that those "things" *don't* make you happy. Warren warns against surrendering "to the opinions or expectations of others, to money, to resentment, to fear, or to your own pride, lusts, or ego. You were designed to worship God, and if you fail to worship Him, you will create other things (idols) to give your life to. You are free to choose what you surrender to, but you are not free from the consequences of that choice." The pleasure-seeking life is a long and lonely road.

Again, there's nothing wrong with pleasure when it comes from a pure source. But it should not be the whole of your goal. When you're living a purpose-driven life, seeking a higher purpose, immersing yourself in something bigger and greater, the pleasure that comes along is a welcome addition. It's like the whipped cream. Your happiness doesn't diminish when hedonic adaptation sets in because pleasure was never the center of your happiness in the first place.

I do need to take a short time out for a little disclaimer here. Have you ever noticed that God pretty much inspires the invention of some pretty cool things to advance the kingdom, and then Satan figures out a way to pervert them? It's like the Internet: You can listen to general conference talks anytime you want, and you can sit at home in your sweats doing family history work. Cool. But Satan couldn't pass on that golden opportunity, so now most of the world has access to all forms of pornography or even get the instructions on how to build a bomb that will kill thousands of people. Elder Jeffrey R. Holland has said, "Tragically, the same computer and Internet service that allows me to do my family history and prepare those names for temple work could, without filters and controls, allow my children or grandchildren access to a global cesspool of perceptions that could blast a crater in their brains forever."

Well, the same thing is true for using your gifts in a cause. When you decide to use your unique gifts in something bigger than yourself, make sure it's also something *greater. Something noble. Something that helps, lifts, and encourages others.* Using your gifts to forward a cause that is selfish and destructive is a twisted version of this important truth.

Intentional Happiness Habits

Even after you have found your own gifts and are using them in a noble cause bigger than yourself, there are more things you can do as part of the intentional activities that make up almost half of your happiness. Let me be clear: these are not the things you do to *create* happiness, but to *add to* and *enhance* your happiness.

Most of these probably sound obvious—really simple, actually. They are. So why do I include them here? Because the obvious things—the simple stuff—can actually be the most profound things you can do. A lot of small and simple things put together can actually create amazing things (where have you heard that before?). And the good news is that you can do the simple stuff without a whole bunch of exertion or inconvenience, yet the simple stuff can actually bring about big returns. I need to be transparent and tell you that causation has not been proven in each of these ten ideas. Each idea has been correlated with happiness, meaning they often go together, but that doesn't necessarily mean that one causes the other. After reading them, however, I think your common sense will tell you that there is a connection between each idea and happiness. I hope you'll agree that each is definitely worth a shot.

The obvious things—the simple stuff—can actually be the most profound things you can do for happiness.

Quick side note: I don't mean these simple steps will cure depression. They won't. They may help, but you really need to work with a professional—a doctor and/or a therapist—and get effective, long-term treatment.

Sound good? Okay, here goes!

Number One: Be Around People Who Are Happy

Being around people who are happy is the number-one way to be happy yourself. It's also the number-one indicator of a person's happiness levels. Why? Simple: happiness is contagious! And unlike the stomach flu, it's something worth catching. In fact, social life and happiness are so closely correlated that they could almost be twins. Think about the people you spend time with. If they're happy, chances are that you're happy too. If they're unhappy, odds are that you are also unhappy.

Happiness is contagious! And unlike the stomach flu, it's something worth catching.

I'm guessing I don't have to spell out any research for you to believe this. I'm sure life has taught you that spending a lot of time around people who are unhappy will definitely impact your happiness. If you're spending much of your time with the neighborhood whiner or the office grouch or the family malcontent, you might need to make some changes. Hold on—I'm not telling you to get rid of anyone in your life. We believe in keeping promises. You shouldn't treat people like cell phones or cars, trading a person in for another model when you get tired of the one you've got. After all, they need friends too, and you can be someone who plays a very positive role in their lives. No need to isolate anyone. If you have someone in your life who is unhappy but who needs to be in your life, that's okay—but bring some happy people in. Spend as much time with happy people as you possibly can.

If most of your friends and associates resemble Eeyore—you know, the droopy eyes, the saggy shuffle, the rain cloud overhead—it might be time to mix it up a bit. And if *you're* the one who resembles Eeyore, then it's *definitely* time to make some changes.

What I *am* saying is that *you need to add more happy people to your life*. Look around. It's pretty easy to tell who the happy people are. They're the ones who are smiling. Who have a sparkle in their eye. Who laugh. Who do fun things (which entails getting up off the couch). Sit by them at church or at community events. Invite some of them into your circle; start to act like them and do the things they do. You'll be amazed at what starts to happen.

Number Two: Spend Money on Other People

As it turns out, money really *can* buy happiness—just not in the way you thought. Dozens of studies have shown that when you take a little of your hard-earned money and spend it to make someone else happy, magical things happen to your own level of happiness.

Money really *can* buy happiness—just not in the way you thought.

Works every time.

Let me share a couple of cool examples, and you'll see how easy it can be. You'll also see that it doesn't take a wad of cash to pull it off. Of course, don't spend money you don't have. Debt, stress, and unhappiness are friends that hang out together. Debt leads to unhappiness in almost every circumstance. We're talking here about spending money you have on others, not spending money you borrowed on others.

When one of my friends missed two consecutive weeks of church meetings because of a bad chest cold, a random woman in the ward showed up at her door. She thrust a little gift bag at my friend, sealed with a hug, as she started to explain. (And you know how women are; the gift bag had all that fancy tissue paper poking out the top and a patterned ribbon to tie it all up.) Inside was a bottle of menthol ointment and a pair of floral socks. It was the key to relief, the woman said: rub the menthol ointment on the soles of your feet before going to bed—in a nice, thick layer, she added—put the socks on over the ointment to hold all the goo in, and voila! A night free of coughing and congestion.

You know what? It worked. So did the happiness—for both of them.

I heard of a single dad who loves to take his kids to a restaurant once a month or so for the express purpose of making someone happy. Once there, they sit at their table and check out all the customers in the place. Together, they identify someone who is eating alone—you know, someone who looks a bit down and out.

And then the fun begins. Enlisting their waiter as their accomplice, they carefully point out the customer and announce that they want to *secretly* pay for that customer's dinner. Secrecy is a big deal here. Dad surreptitiously slides his credit card to the waiter, who quietly goes to the back and takes care of the bill.

The whole family subtly watches as the lucky diner-o'-the-night learns that his meal has been paid for. The family nearly bursts with glee—undercover, of course—as the diner eagerly glances around the restaurant, trying to figure out who would have done such a thing. Believe me when I tell you it's one of the highlights of the month for the family, and it always puts a smile on the face and a spring in the step of the lucky diner as well.

Happiness all around for nothing more than the cost of a meal. Heck, even the waiter probably gets a happiness surge out of the whole thing.

It's not very difficult to give this a try. Run down to the store and buy a random gift for someone in your life. Not overly expensive—just an expression of appreciation. Pay attention to how you feel. My guess is that your internal happiness meter is going to bump up a couple of notches.

Speaking of money, here's a shocker: If you want to be happy, all you actually need is money sufficient for your needs.

That's right: lots of research accompanied by astute observation proves that once you're above the poverty level and make enough to provide for your needs, any money above that has an *extremely insignificant* impact on your happiness.

Let's put it another way, punctuated by some cold, hard numbers. Let's say you live in the United States and you make $75,000 a year. In terms of your happiness level, the difference between that scenario and one in which you make $1.5 million a year is statistically insignificant. At that level, more money will not make you any happier.

No way, you're thinking. *That* can't *be right.* I remember telling that to one woman who quipped, "Those people just don't know where to shop." Another said, "Yeah, but I'd be unhappy in some very nice places."

Well, think again. And here's why it works like that: too many of us have been conditioned to think that happiness equates to wealth. The Savior called it "the deceitfulness of riches" (Matthew 13:22). Some may think and even preach that the high you get when you buy something new is the end-all, be-all of happiness. It's plainly and simply not true. Don't work your entire life chasing money only to find out you were on the wrong path.

> Too many of us think that happiness equates to wealth. Don't work your entire life chasing money only to find out you were on the wrong path.

Don't get me wrong. No one likes to be on a budget so tight it screams with pain. No one enjoys being unable to get an ice-cream cone on the way home. No one likes volleying calls from bill collectors. That's why it's important to have *sufficient for your needs.* But beyond that? Not necessary. Not for happiness, anyway. Time to drop the myth.

Number Three: Cut Down on Screen Time

Screens, whether they be ninety-inch plasmas or three-inch phones, can be wonderful tools. I love my phone! It seems to make my life so much easier. But while my phone is a wonderful device, it is a horrible master.

There is nothing inherently evil about a screen, just like there is nothing inherently evil about pizza or candy. However, if I ate pizza and candy four to five hours a day, you can bet it wouldn't be long before I started having problems.

Many studies have confirmed that too much screen time has damaging effects on the brain structure and function. Screen time has been correlated to depression and anxiety time and again, study after study. Gaming and Internet addictions have been tied to shrinkage of brain matter, impacting the parts of the brain that control emotion and relationship skills. One study found that too much screen time resulted in an insensitivity to loss, while another found that too much screen time resulted in interrupted communication between the two hemispheres of the brain (commonly called "right" and "left").

What exactly is it about screens that causes these problems? Scientists aren't sure. Some say it is disrupted sleep, some say it is overloaded sensory systems, some say it is the reduction in physical activity, and others say it is the limited personal connections. The exact causes are still unknown, but there is sufficient evidence to start taking steps to limit screen time for ourselves and our children.

Number Four: Talk to People. In Person.

Seriously? Yes. Absolutely.

It's something that's easy to do, that doesn't cost a cent, and that doesn't require a how-to manual—yet it can be a sizable contributor to your happiness. And here's all there is to it: have deep, in-person conversations with the important people in your life.

Okay—there are always times when you need to talk on the phone, or text, or IM, or Facebook, or Skype, or use whatever swanky high-tech tools are at your fingertips. Sometimes our early ancestors were reduced to using smoke signals or sending carrier pigeons. Just make sure that's not *all* you do. Take the time and make the effort to really engage people, eye to eye. You can start with the dinner table and go from there.

Why? Happy people emotionally connect with other people in real life. Emotional connections with others really help the brain. And the best way to emotionally connect is to *talk*, face-to-face. Go for a hike, go for a walk, go to lunch—it doesn't matter where you go, just talk to another human being. It will make a difference in your happiness.

And if you've got youth in your home, make a special point of giving them practice in this critical skill. Ever watched a group of kids huddled together, each one texting on a cell phone? They need practice in face-to-face communication—and you can be the one to give them that practice.

Number Five: Laugh!

Happy people laugh. If you want to be happier, laugh. A lot.

I remember an executive who told the story of being in a high-powered meeting with a bunch of people who were her bosses. She, of course, was focused on making the best impression humanly possible when all of a sudden she opened her mouth to make what would have been a stunningly impressive statement. At that very second, the crown on her front tooth flew out of her mouth like a heat-seeking missile and bounced across the glass-topped conference table. There she sat, looking like a cast member from *The Beverly Hillbillies.*

You can bet everyone at that table—including her—lost every shred of interest in what she had been about to say. And you can bet that everyone at that table—other than her—uttered a silent prayer of gratitude for the skill of their dentists.

And her? She laughed. Hard. And once she was genuinely laughing, so was everyone else at the table.

Every time she tells that story, she still laughs. So do all the people she tells it to. Because she is one of the happiest women around, even with a missing front tooth.

So which comes first, happiness or laughter? This seems to be another chicken-or-the-egg deal. Maybe laughing makes you happy. Maybe being happy makes you laugh. No one really knows if one causes the other, but we do know that they are correlated. They come and go together.

Laughter is very good for you. They knew that clear back in biblical times: Solomon, hailed for his wisdom, remarked that "a merry heart doeth good like a medicine" (Proverbs 17:22). Throughout the ages and around the world, members of royal courts valued the court jester, the colorful clown who made them laugh and in the bargain helped them tolerate the job of governing.

One thirteenth-century surgeon told jokes to his patients on their way out of surgery, knowing that the ones who laughed recovered better. A sixteenth-century English educator prescribed laughter for those afflicted with head colds; a favorite "cure" was being tickled in the armpits. (Try *that* next time you have a cold.) Humor was even used by ancient Americans—Ojibway Indian doctor-clowns used laughter to heal the sick.

I'm not the only one who says that laughter is good for you. Studies published in the *Journal of the American Medical Association* say that laughing clears mucus from the lungs, increases the amount of oxygen that circulates through the blood, conditions your muscles, provides muscle relaxation, speeds up circulation, and increases the amount of oxygen delivered to all your body cells. Laughter has even been proven in scientific studies to relieve pain and boost your immunity. Perhaps it's time to choose the comedy over the drama in the movie theater this weekend?

Just twenty seconds of laughter is the cardiovascular equivalent of three minutes of strenuous rowing.

And for all you exercise enthusiasts, consider this: Stanford Medical School psychiatrist William Fry Jr. says that just twenty seconds of laughter is the cardiovascular equivalent of three minutes of strenuous rowing. In fact, he said, it took him *ten minutes* on a rowing machine to get his heart to the rate it was at after just *one minute* of hearty laughter. Other experts have said that the changes laughter causes in your body are so effective that laughter may be classified as aerobic exercise. The best part of all? You don't have to go to the gym or run around a track or use a fancy machine to laugh. All you need is a sense of humor.

But laughter does much more than help you physically. It also reduces stress and improves your perspective on all kinds of things—even things that are as real and distressing as pain. Best of all, *it enhances happiness.* It's one of the simplest things you can do to improve your level of happiness.

If you need some inspiration, watch children. Children laugh, on average, upward of three hundred times per day. Adults? Fifteen times per day. What happened? Was it the mortgage? Whatever it was, don't allow yourself to turn into that grumpy neighbor you were scared of as a kid.

So laugh every chance you get. Make sure it's appropriate. Never laugh at sacred things or take sacred things lightly, something you may recognize as "loud laughter." Also, watch out for what I call "cheap laughter"—laughing at crude things. Cheap laughter isn't witty or intelligent—it's like cheap fast food that gives you stomach cramps. Intelligent humor is like the mouthwatering food at a five-star restaurant.

Lastly, never laugh *at* someone. I've never seen a moment where cruelty was remotely funny. Laughing that bullies or demeans another person will cause the Spirit to withdraw. And when the Spirit withdraws, say good-bye to any real happiness.

But laughing at yourself and your own awkwardness, like our toothless friend did, is perfectly okay. And if you're out of practice, check out some funny movies or talks or books, or go get a shake with the funniest person you know.

Number Six: Listen to Uplifting Music

Uplifting music has a significant impact on happiness.

Don't just take my word for it. I have proof!

Some researchers wanted to know if music really did affect happiness, so they decided to test it. They gathered up two groups of volunteers. One spent an hour a day for three months listening to uplifting music—they got to choose the music, but it had to be uplifting. Probably no greatest hits from Nine-Inch Pumpkin Smashing Megadeath.

The other group got an hour-long massage every day for three months. I know. Sign me up.

At the end of three months, they interviewed and tested both groups of people. Hang on to your hats, because the group with the highest level of happiness was the one that listened to uplifting music every day. The music, not the massage, had the greatest effect on happiness. (When I read these findings, of course, I was thinking we should combine the two—listen to an hour of uplifting music while having an hour-long massage. Now *that* could cause sheer bliss!)

Even without the massage, the message is clear: Uplifting music makes you happy. Have your uplifting playlist ready for when you are feeling down.

Number Seven: Exercise and Eat a Healthy Diet

You undoubtedly already know this, and you undoubtedly don't want to hear it again. It might just be one of the most overused pieces of advice on the planet. In fact, it might make you want to throw up in your mouth a little.

Believe me: I *wouldn't* say it if it wasn't completely true. The fact is that happy people exercise and eat a healthy diet.

Let me make one thing perfectly clear here: the happiness you get from exercising and eating a healthy diet has *nothing* to do with your body weight, shape, or size. It's not about that at all. It's not about how you *look*. Don't believe me? After all, you've seen the ads. If you've got flawless skin and bouncy hair and a size-four waist, you're going to be happy—right? Wrong. You mean that being prettier is not going to make you happier? Nope.

I'm not saying that just because I haven't won any beauty competitions—not even the ones in which I was the only contestant. I'm saying it because cold, hard research backs it up. One study compared some really good-looking people with some who weren't all that good-looking. And guess what? Neither group was happier than the other. It's obvious that a gazillion dollars' worth of beauty products are hanging by the hair of their chinny-chin-chins on trying to convince you that just the opposite is true, but believe me here. Happiness doesn't hang on your looks.

But we digress. A large study involving a group of women measured their happiness levels after exercising every day. I'm not talking training for marathons—I'm talking getting out every day for a walk. The ones whose happiness levels increased the most were those who got out and walked every day. And the boost in happiness didn't hinge on whether they lost weight or dropped a dress size or two. It hinged on getting some exercise.

And now for the *D* word: diet. The neurotransmitters in your brain that are responsible for creating and maintaining happiness depend on the food you put in your body. Now, your mouth may be very happy with some Ding Dongs or a Mountain Dew. But your brain, the place where it's all happening, might as well be starving to death, calorie counts notwithstanding. Ding Dongs and a Mountain Dew simply don't give your brain much to go on.

Your mouth may be very happy with some Ding Dongs or a Mountain Dew. But your brain, the place where it's all happening, might as well be starving to death.

What *should* you be eating, then? The list is right at your fingertips: D&C 89. Shocking, I know, but the Word of Wisdom is pretty right on. Fruit, nuts, vegetables, protein—it's what the brain needs to keep you feeling happy. Too many refined sugars and empty calories can be tough for your body to convert into any brain energy. By this point, you're probably good at avoiding the bad stuff, so try reading the Lord's directive and looking for the *good* stuff.

Number Eight: Go Outside a Lot

Happy people go outside a lot.

Are they happy because they go outside? Or do they go outside because they're happy? Once again, as you've already read in this chapter, no one knows. Correlation and causation are sometimes super tricky. All you need to know is that happiness and going outside go hand in hand. It's worth a shot, right?

Before you read any more, let's define *outside*. *Outside* doesn't mean looking out the window while you're doing the dishes and thinking, *Wow, it really is pretty outside today.* Nope, that's not outside. *Outside* doesn't mean driving to work and looking out through the windshield. *Outside* doesn't mean that minute-long walk through the parking lot from the car into the grocery store. *Outside* also doesn't mean watching a screen with people who are outside. None of those qualifies as *outside*.

What am I talking about, then? I'm talking about spending some quality time—you know, twenty or thirty minutes at a whack—outside in the fresh air. In nature, as God designed it. Here's an idea: instead of sitting inside on your couch while you read, set up a chair outside on the deck or on the grass or on the patio and read out there. If you're really brave, you could just sit on the grass—as long as you're sure you can get back up unassisted. Breathe in the fresh air. Feel the warmth of the sun (or the cool of the shade). Smell the flowers and shrubs in your garden. Studies show that surgery patients recover faster and need fewer medications when they spend time outside.

Here's another bit of research for you to chew on: the happiest families go camping. That's right—*camping*. There's just something about being in the great outdoors, making s'mores over the campfire, falling asleep to the orchestra of crickets that contributes to happiness. And we haven't even started talking about riding rugged trails on an ATV.

If the idea of pitching a tent and rolling around on the hard ground in a stuffy sleeping bag while swatting at mosquitoes makes you anything but happy, go hotel camping: sleep at the hotel, and spend the day outside doing fun things with your family. It doesn't matter where you sleep. It matters how much time you spend outside.

Believe me when I say that outside is where it's at. Nature is very accepting of all of us. It doesn't care what you look like or how much money you make. There's no judgment there. In all the time I've spent outside, I've never had a tree turn away from me with its nose in the air when I walk by. Trees like you no matter what. Nature seems to provide us with energy, intrinsic worth, and vitality. Go take a walk, my friend.

Number Nine: Get Enough Sleep

Happy people get enough sleep.

Sleep is important to all kinds of things, including happiness. But it doesn't stop there. Did you know that your body heals only when you are sleeping? That's why you feel totally wasted when you get a bad cold or the flu: it's your body's way of telling you that you need to *go to sleep* so it can get on with its job of healing.

You may not have known that, but I'm *sure* you know this: People who don't get enough sleep are crabby. There's not a person alive who hasn't gone head-to-head with a sleep-deprived grump. When you don't get enough sleep, nothing works as it should. And it's very tough to be happy under those conditions. One study even showed that healthy sleep is correlated with how much money you'll make.

When it comes to sleep, our culture has made a fascinating shift in the last three or four centuries. In medieval times, it was a hassle to get much light in the house after dark; I mean, you can only burn so many candles. So when it got dark, people went to sleep. Face it: there wasn't much work you could get done after the sun went down. When the sun came up again the next morning, people were up and at it again. In between, there was plenty of time for quality shut-eye. Sleep was seen as a friend, a nurse.

Then along came Thomas Edison and the lightbulb, and before you knew it, lighting up the house anytime of day or night was as easy as flipping a switch. Suddenly people didn't go to sleep as soon as it got dark. In fact, Edison blew off sleep as a complete waste of time. He thought the lights should never be turned off at all. "Edison spent considerable amounts of his own and his staff's energy on publicizing the idea that success depended in no small part in staying awake to stay ahead of the technological and economic competition."[1]

That's not all. Edison was willing to work "at all hours, night or day," to rack up more than a hundred hours of work in a week. And he chose his employees based largely on their physical endurance—if *he* slept only three or four hours a night, he expected the same of

---

[1] Alan Derickson, *Dangerously Sleepy: Overworked Americans and the Cult of Manly Wakefulness* (University of Pennsylvania Press, 2013).

them. Oh, and don't think they ever pulled one over on old Tom. When employees started dozing off under stairways or in corners, Edison hired "watchers" to nab them and pull them back onto the production floor.[2] I'm not sure Edison understood how unique he was in the way his brain worked. He was able to work hard and stay positive (we are going to talk about his gift for positivity later) on very little sleep—that's not true for most of us.

People who need sleep are *not* softies. They're what scientists call "alive." They're human beings.

And that brings us to today, where we keep the midnight oil burning so we can get just one more thing done . . . and one more . . . and one more. And before we know it, we're burning the candle at both ends. That doesn't impact just our happiness—it also deals a massive punch to our physical and mental well-being. And here's the worst part: some people (and you may know some of them, if you're not one yourself) are actually *proud* of the fact that they short-change themselves on sleep. "For some, sleep loss is a badge of honor, a sign that they don't require the eight-hour biological reset that the rest of us softies do. Others feel that keeping up with peers requires sacrifice at the personal level—and at least in the short-term, sleep is an invisible sacrifice."[3]

Well, I'm here to tell you that people who need sleep are *not* softies. They're what scientists call "alive." They're human beings. And that includes you, and it includes me. If you have a regular time when you need to wake up and it's complete torture to pull yourself off the mattress, try going to sleep earlier.

Not everyone requires the same amount of sleep. Some get by just fine on five hours, and others really do need ten. Everyone is different. There are lots of ways to tell if you're getting enough sleep.

---

[2] Olga Khazan, "Thomas Edison and the Cult of Sleep Deprivation," *The Atlantic*, May 2014.

[3] Khazan.

If you doze off on the toilet, you're probably not getting enough sleep. If you pass out during the staff meeting at work, you're probably not getting enough sleep (that, or you might work with the lamest group of lemmings on the planet). If you can't watch your favorite half-hour sitcom or read a magazine article without starting to drool, you're probably not getting enough sleep.

To find out for sure, try this experiment. Go to sleep *without* setting your alarm, and see when you wake up. If you wake up at about your usual time, you're likely getting enough sleep. If you're still snoring contentedly away hours after you usually get up, you're probably sleep-deprived and need more shut-eye than you're getting. Once you've figured that out, figure out how to work it so you can get to bed earlier. You have to be intentional about it. As you've heard countless times: Act. Don't just be acted upon.

Number Ten: Tune in to the Spiritual

Here's my favorite of all ten: Happy people are spiritual.

Notice I didn't say that happy people are *religious*. There's a big difference between being spiritual and being religious (which is often measured by how often you go to church . . . although I hope that people who go to church are happier too).

One of the ways you can increase your spirituality is through meditation—which, not coincidentally, has a huge impact on happiness. Before you panic, I'm not talking about sitting cross-legged on a rug in your room surrounded by candles and inhaling incense.

Here's what I *am* talking about: Either sit in a chair or kneel on the floor, whichever works best for you. (Kneeling? Seems like the Lord had something there.) Now think deeply, staying focused on single thoughts one at a time.

Hey, wait! you may be thinking, *that sounds a lot like prayer.* Indeed it does. And our Heavenly Father knew it would make us all happier to talk to Him every day, to report on what's happening in our lives. Obviously, He already knows what's happening in our lives, but it fills our happiness quotient to tell Him anyway. Kneel, breathe, go slow, focus, think, ponder, create mental plans—really communicate with the Lord.

Here's another way to tune in to the spiritual, though I know it might not work for everyone—and I want you to know that I say it completely without judgment. First, let me set the stage: I made a CD several years ago called *Break Up with the World*. You can get it wherever fine LDS products are . . . Oh, oops. Back to the story. So this CD was about breaking up with things that are affecting you negatively—you know, like breaking up with a bad boyfriend. Sure, it's hard. Chances are you'll miss him really terribly at first, but after awhile you won't even think about him anymore. That's how it works.

Well, about ten years ago, we broke up with television.

You read that right. We kept the TV around to occasionally watch DVDs, but our television time was cut dramatically. We went from an hour or two a day to an hour or two a month. Yup, it was hard. We missed it—especially at first, but after a while we didn't even think about it anymore. Just like a bad boyfriend.

Last year, for some reason, we decided we just *had* to watch the Olympics. And we wanted our kids to be able to watch the Olympics. Go figure. So we either had to hang out in restaurants that were broadcasting the Olympics from dawn to dusk, or we had to somehow get access to television. So we took what we figured was the high road: we bought a program that lets us watch actual television on our computer.

Ba-da-bing: *television was back in our home*! Because, of course, there were all those commercials for all *sorts* of things during the Olympics. It took awhile for me to explain to my children what commercials were—they couldn't figure out why the Olympics kept getting interrupted. And, of course, it didn't stop at the Olympics. We were drawn to other programs. To put it simply, the bad boyfriend was back.

The result? There was an absolute, noticeable difference in the feeling of spirituality and the happiness level in our home almost the same day the television leaped out through the computer screen. It was unreal. Television proved to be one of the connections to the world that impacted our happiness. It was a breakup that was quickly made permanent.

Now maybe television isn't the thing that has a negative influence on your family and on your family's spirituality and happiness. But look around for the things that *are*. Notice—*really notice*—what comes into your home through the magazines you read, the music you and your family listen to, the things you watch on television, the stuff you access on the Internet. What disrupts your spiritual feelings and impressions? If there's something you decide deserves a breakup, take a stand. Set the limits that help you start breaking your connections with the world.

Your spirituality will soar, and so will your happiness.

Take a tip from me: don't try to tackle all ten of these at once. Don't even try to tackle *two* of them at once. Instead, choose *one*. Most of the energy you need to make a change is in this initial phase. It's like the space shuttle: most of the energy occurs during the launch. Once the shuttle is launched into orbit, it's pretty much set. And that's how it is with change: most of the energy you need to accomplish change happens in the first two or three weeks. Focus on one thing at a time.

I hope by now you have a basic understanding of happiness and an idea of what does and doesn't cause it. But there's much more—so please keep reading.

CHAPTER TWO

"Whose Fruit Was Desirable to Make One Happy": What the Scriptures Teach about Happiness

BELIEVE IT OR NOT, IF you want one of the best educations on happiness in all the world, just pick up the Book of Mormon.

For one thing, it tells us what this life is all about: Lehi taught his son Jacob, "Men are, that they might have joy" (2 Nephi 2:25). In other words, that's our *purpose*. Having joy. Or, in other words, being happy. But thank heaven the Book of Mormon doesn't stop there. It goes on to tell us *how* to achieve happiness.

And here's a fun little aside: it's done in a bit of a veiled way.

Here's how President Henry B. Eyring describes it: "The Lord has embedded in [the Book of Mormon] His message to you . . . and those who put it together [Mormon, Moroni, and Nephi] put in messages for you."[4]

How cool is *that*? The Lord *embedded* His message in the Book of Mormon! Let's look at what that means: as you read along, you can find totally awesome messages tucked into the stories we all know—messages that can change your life. They're marching along in the lines of text right there for anyone who's looking.

It's kind of like the *Da Vinci Code*, but even better—the *Mormon Code*!

Mormon, Moroni, and Nephi are the ones who put together the Book of Mormon, and they knew what they were doing with all those embedded messages. Mormon was the absolute best—he had this gift of embedding principles into stories so well that you don't even know you're learning principles. You think you're just reading stories. Never read the Book of Mormon without asking yourself, "What's the embedded message here?"

[4] Henry B. Eyring, "The Book of Mormon Will Change Your Life," *Liahona*, February 2004, 15.

There are all kinds of messages embedded in the Book of Mormon, including the principles of happiness. Two chapters in particular—2 Nephi 5 and 4 Nephi 1—contain clear messages that will lead us to increased happiness if we find those messages and are willing to live by them.

First, a little background to 2 Nephi 5. Both Nephi and Laman were born to and raised by the same parents. Both had to flee from Jerusalem and tramp through the wilderness—thorns, snakes, marauders, and all, not to mention those cumbersome tents. Both had to put up with the struggles of drifting across the sea to the promised land in a boat built by their brother, a guy who had *never before built a boat*. Both had to set themselves up in uncharted territory with nothing more than what they brought on the boat. Simply put, Nephi and Laman satisfy both the "nature" and the "nurture" camp: same biology, same environment.

What happened next? In spite of all the hoopla involved in running for their lives and trying to find the promised land and starting all over in a new place, Nephi proclaimed, "It came to pass that we lived after the manner of happiness" (2 Nephi 5:27).

At least, that's how *Nephi* and *his* followers felt.

But Laman didn't see it that way exactly. He didn't seem to have a happy bone in his body. He was so unhappy, in fact, that he frequently became unhinged and wanted to kill Nephi and sometimes Sam and Lehi. Not what you'd call a well-balanced individual.

After Lehi passed away, it was time to choose sides. The Lord gave Nephi some advance info, warning him that Laman and Lemuel were out for blood and that he should flee into the wilderness (again!) with everyone who would go along (see 2 Nephi 5:5). Nephi, being the obedient guy that he was, took those who believed in the Lord and fled into the wilderness, even though he'd just barely made that same sort of trip. (Why don't the bad guys ever have to flee?) The result was two separate groups. And that's how we got Nephites and Lamanites. Personal decisions can have consequences reaching far beyond our own lives (that was an embedded principle).

Even with all that gloom and doom, Nephi still felt happy—and 2 Nephi 5 gives us an encoded pattern of happiness we can follow in our own lives. We'll examine that pattern later in this chapter.

Now a little background on 4 Nephi 1, the other chapter that gives us great embedded messages about happiness. You remember: the Savior had just visited the Nephites, and the prophet-historian Mormon described the people by writing, "There could not be a happier people among all the people who had been created by the hand of God" (4 Nephi 1:16). *All the people who had been created by God?* That's quite a statement. In my opinion, Mormon is saying, "If you want to be happy, do what they did!"

We're also told in the second verse that throughout the entire land—including among those once-bloodthirsty Lamanites—"there were no contentions and disputations among them, and every man did deal justly one with another" (4 Nephi 1:2).

Now that you understand the two chapters, you are ready for some digging. I'll guide you along, since you're just getting started. I'll show you seven of the embedded messages these two chapters contain on how to achieve lasting happiness, and as I do, you'll see how to spot those messages for yourself.

Keep the Commandments

What do we learn about these two very happy groups of people? After Nephi got the lead out and put some intense distance between him and his two brothers, he described how his people—you know, the ones who lived "after the manner of happiness"—conducted themselves. "And we did observe to keep the judgments, and the statutes, and the commandments of the Lord in all things," he wrote (2 Nephi 5:10).

And what about the band of people who had been visited by the Savior—the ones who were happier than all the people ever created? We are told that "they did walk after the commandments which they had received from their Lord and their God, continuing in fasting and prayer, and in meeting together oft both to pray and to hear the word of the Lord" (4 Nephi 1:12).

Okay. These messages aren't too deeply embedded. In fact, they're in-your-face obvious. But in case you missed them, let me be perfectly clear, no encryption involved: *keeping the commandments is your best shot for lasting happiness in this life*. Keeping the commandments is not a guarantee that you won't have trials. There are no guarantees like that, because as we've already discussed, this life is designed to create problems for you to work through. But keeping the commandments gives you the very best bet for happiness, no matter what happens in your life. The commandments lead to happiness, which is why God gave them.

Keeping the commandments gives you the very best bet for happiness, no matter what happens in your life.

The same message is embedded in shallow waters elsewhere in the Book of Mormon. You're undoubtedly familiar with Alma 41:10, which warns that "wickedness never was happiness." Or how about Helaman 13:38, when Samuel the Lamanite tells a people about to be destroyed that "ye have sought for happiness in doing iniquity, which thing is contrary to the nature of [God]." Growing happiness from seeds of disobedience is impossible. C.S. Lewis said it this way: "God cannot give us a happiness and peace apart from Himself, because it is not there. There is no such thing."

One of the smartest and best characters in the Book of Mormon, King Benjamin, encouraged his people to "consider on the blessed and happy state of those that keep the commandments of God" (Mosiah 2:41). Benjamin had seen a lot in his day—had been around the block a time or two, so to say. He'd seen people who were miserably unhappy and people who were blessedly happy, and he knew what made the difference. The happy ones kept the commandments of God. Do what King Benjamin asked and consider that for a minute.

Why can't you break the commandments and be happy? One reason is that it's *really* hard to be happy when you believe one thing and do another. Serving two masters leads to a whole lot of internal conflict. Indian spiritual and political leader Mahatma Gandhi spelled it out pretty plainly when he wrote, "Happiness is when what you think, what you say, and what you do are in harmony."

You can't believe the words of Christ or the commandments of God and then expect to be happy if you blow them off. Obedience to the commandments brings peace of mind and peace of conscience, two sure-fire ingredients of happiness.

And as you've now read from the pages of the Book of Mormon, happiness in sin is impossible.

Wait a minute, you may be thinking. *I have a friend* (or sister, or cousin, or employer, or neighbor, or coworker, or child—or what about those Hollywood celebrities) *who is perfectly happy, and I* know *she isn't keeping the commandments.* Sure. We all know one of those. You might know lots of them. Genuine happiness isn't found at the end of a vodka bottle, and authentic joy isn't found in an illicit sexual relationship or in spending more money than you make. Those things may bring temporary, carnal pleasure or some kind of high, but they will never bring the kind of lasting happiness we all desire. Instead, they often bring painful regret—it's cheap pleasure with an aftertaste. To be fair, perhaps for someone who doesn't know about the commandments, carnal experiences are all they understand about happiness. That's not their fault. We know that everyone born on the planet has the Light of Christ—the uplifting influence many call conscience. Therefore, whether the person be a member of the Church or not, happiness comes from living correct principles. The more correct principles you live, the happier you become. Commandment breaking, no matter who does it, can't lead to happiness. That would be like trying to grow apples on a peach tree. The owner of the tree may tell you they are apples, and he might even believe that they are apples, but nothing in the world can make them apples. It's simply impossible.

Focus on the Temple

What else do we learn from those people who lived "after the manner of happiness"? A major message is embedded in 2 Nephi 5:16, in which Nephi tells us simply that he "did build a temple."

To be honest with you, I laughed about that verse for years—not because Nephi built a temple, but because what he tells us in that same verse about the process of building that temple: "I did construct it after the manner of the temple of Solomon save it were not built of so many precious things; for they were not to be found upon the land, wherefore, it could not be built like unto Solomon's temple. But the manner of the construction was like unto the temple of Solomon."

I always wanted to yell, "Nephi, make up your mind!" It was like Nephi was saying, "I built a temple; it was like Solomon's temple. Oh, wait, no it wasn't. Oh, wait, yes it was!" I could never figure out why he was arguing with himself in that verse. I even considered a time or two—put up your lightning rod here—that it was sort of a waste of space on plates that were pretty tough to engrave on to begin with.

But that all changed when a student provided me with a whole new outlook on verse sixteen. As I started to laugh about it in my by-now-customary way, she cut me off with a startling declaration: "I *love* that verse!"

"*Really*?" I asked. I think she could see I was skeptical. I was about to ask, "Is that the only verse you've read?"

Then she explained. "Nephi wants to do his best, but there are certain materials he has no access to, so he does the best he can. I love that verse because my dad's not a member of the Church; he's not even a good person. I look at my friends, and they all have righteous dads, and I don't. I could put all my focus on what I don't have—you know, a righteous dad is not to be found upon my land—but instead, I'm going to make my life the very best I can with the materials I have."

Wow! I thought, *Why am I teaching this class? She should be up in front.*

I want to give you just a little more insight about the construction of a very particular temple. Those of you who have visited the Manhattan New York Temple will know exactly what I'm talking about. My brother-in-law was a Secret Service agent—but don't tell, it's secret—stationed in Manhattan for five years, so we had the chance to visit a number of times. Manhattan is an amazing city filled with so much history, and I love it there. It's also a loud city—and I mean there's noise everywhere, all the time, and I love it!

The first time my brother-in-law drove us by the temple, he pointed to a building on the corner of Columbus Avenue and told us all, "There's the temple!"

Sure enough, right next to the sidewalk, practically right in the street, was the temple. What came out of my mouth right then was not my finest moment: "Where is the grass? There's no grass? What about the trees?"

At that split second, I also became acutely aware of all the noise around me—squealing brakes, honking horns, deafening music, and the uproar of throngs of people. It scarcely seemed conducive to the reverence I associate with a temple. Why on earth would they have put a *temple* just a few feet away from some of the loudest commotion on earth? As if he could read my mind, my brother said, "It's totally silent in the celestial room, you know."

No, I didn't know. And how was that even humanly possible? There are buses and taxis not more than ten feet from the temple's walls. There is a reason nobody wants to live right next to a busy highway.

Here's how: It all hinges on the way the temple was built. The temple was built *inside* an existing building, and the interior temple walls are connected to the outer building walls at only a few critical junctures. The temple isn't connected to the outside world. This too is a great lesson for us on how to be happy: limit the extent to which the outside world touches and influences our lives. How connected are you to the "noise" of the world? Do you allow offensive television shows, movies, music, websites—or anything else that show people living out of the *For the Strength of Satan* pamphlet—into your life? That type of media will affect your happiness.

> The temple isn't connected to the outside world. This is a great lesson on how to be happy: limit the extent to which the outside world touches and influences your life.

Back to that embedded message in which Nephi built a temple. Happiness is inseparable from temple blessings. The temple is where we learn that a loving Heavenly Father created this incredible planet for us, where we are taught the plan to become more like Him, and where we are reminded of why we are on earth. The temple unlocks our God-given gifts, and there we promise to use them in His service. We see clearly that we have a great purpose in His plan.

When we attend the temple, we feel our Father's power, presence, and approval. We feel closer to Him. We learn about Him and the Savior through countless symbols. It's difficult to imagine a greater source of joy and happiness. Even if we can't attend the temple on a regular basis, having a picture of the temple in our home and a current temple recommend in our wallet are powerful reminders of what we have learned and experienced there.

Happiness is inseparable from temple blessings.

Belong to a Family

The next thing we learn about Nephi's people is that they "began to prosper exceedingly" (2 Nephi 5:13). He's not just talking about material blessings. He is also referring to the same thing that was happening among the Saints at Bountiful following the Savior's visit: the people "were married, and given in marriage" (4 Nephi 1:11).

In fact, they didn't just get married. Check out this additional embedded message: the people of Nephi "did multiply exceedingly fast" (4 Nephi 1:10). That doesn't mean they were in math class. They were having children!

Could it be that marrying and having children is a key to happiness? The Lord's servants seem to think so. In his general conference address of October 1977, President James E. Faust said, "Happiness in marriage and parenthood can exceed a thousand times any other happiness." And he's not the only one: lots of scientific research shows that married people tend to be happier than unmarried people. I know, I know—there are obvious exceptions to that, as demonstrated by the divorce rates in this country. But the general rule is that the married folks are happier. Not only that, they enjoy better health and live longer lives.

This might be a chicken-and-the-egg deal. Which came first? Do you need to be happy in order to get married? Or does happiness make a good marriage? Or do good marriages create happiness? I don't know the answer to that. In fact, no one does. But here's one thing on which most of the research agrees: there is a definite correlation between being married and being happy. As many in the world move further and further away from valuing marriage and family, you may start to believe the lie that getting married and having children will take away from your happiness. You might even think, "I want freedom. I want to travel. I don't want to be tied down to anyone. I'll be happier unmarried and never having children." That is a lie. Getting married and having children will be a significant source of happiness that enriches and blesses your life more than you can possibly imagine.

Hold on. So if you've never had the opportunity to marry, or you've not had the chance to have children, does that mean you're staring right down the barrel at the missing link to happiness?

No. Not at all.

If you're not married or you don't have children, you can tremendously boost your happiness level by having good relationships with other family members—you know, your parents, siblings, grandparents, even those cousins hanging out on the far branches of your family tree. Who doesn't have a favorite uncle or aunt? Even close friends often become "like family." You can experience great happiness by offering each person in your family—whomever that family consists of—your friendship, understanding, and love. As you enjoy these crucial relationships, believe that the Lord has a purpose in your personal plan of happiness. Believe that the happy marriage and family that has been withheld from you will be yours in God's own time. Faith in the Lord includes faith in the Lord's timing.

And consider what you get in return from being part of a family: physical safety, emotional fulfillment, and a sense of belonging. All of which—studies have shown—are essential to experiencing happiness. Again, it's as if the Lord knew all this before scientists figured it out.

Be United

Let's move on to a couple of embedded messages that are a bit more tricky to decipher. As Nephi fled into the wilderness after hearing the Lord's alert, he sized up those who were fleeing with him and reported that they "believed in the warnings and the revelations of God" (2 Nephi 5:6). Then as Nephi settled down after leaving Laman and Lemuel in the dust, he said, "And all those who were with me did take upon them to call themselves the people of Nephi" (2 Nephi 5:9).

The message here? Nephi was surrounded by people who were united in their faith. There were no divisions among them. They were all one people. That's a big embedded principle of happiness right there.

Now let's look at the people who had been visited by the Savior, who offer up the same clue: "There were no robbers, nor murderers, neither were there Lamanites, nor any manner of -ites; but they were in one, the children of Christ, and heirs to the kingdom of God" (4 Nephi 1:17).

This is a hard one. You can't exactly round up all the people in your neighborhood or community or workplace and demand that they see things exactly like you do—that they feel the same or behave the same way you do. That's a one-way ticket to becoming the least popular person on the block. Besides, that's not what Nephi or the people in 4 Nephi did.

So what *does* it mean? It means that you take care in building your close social circle. It means that you spend the most time with people who believe as you do. Who strengthen your faith. Whose presence is uplifting. Who set a good example. Who encourage you to do the things you know are right. It's hard to fall when you are surrounded by so many upstanding people. It has been said that you will become just like the people you spend the most time with. Choose to spend time with people who are what you want to become.

Sometimes we don't realize exactly how important that is—but those interactions have a significant impact on our happiness. Sociologist Christine Carter of the University of California at Berkeley wrote, "The quantity and quality of a person's social connections—friendships, relationships with family members, closeness to neighbors, etc.—is so closely related to well-being and personal happiness the two can practically be equated."[5]

---

5 Christine Carter, "Happiness Is Being Socially Connected," October 31, 2008, greatergood.berkeley.edu.

And while you're building your social circle, think about the -ites. If you want to be united, there can be no -ites, just as the people of Nephi experienced. During the time I taught seminary, I used to notice this "-ites" phenomenon especially among teenagers. You've seen them: The popular-ites. The nonpopular-ites. The modest-ites. The jock-ites. The antijock-ites. The cheerleader-ites. The dance-ites. The academic-ites. The prude-ites. Maybe you've experienced them, even as an adult—the rich-ites, the poor-ites, the BMW-ites, the active-ites, the healthfood-ites, the my-kids-are-smarter-than-your-kids-ites.

If you're going to be *one*—going to experience the greatest happiness—do your part to avoid creating any of those -ites in your social circle. Work to make sure everyone feels included.

Work Hard

Nephi's new little colony did something else that enabled them to live "after the manner of happiness." In 2 Nephi 5:11 and 15, Nephi tells us that his people planted and harvested crops, worked with various ores, built buildings, and raised animals. None of that stuff was designed for the faint of heart. And wrapping it all up, he told us this: "I, Nephi, did cause my people to be industrious, and to labor with their hands" (2 Nephi 5:17).

And what about the band of Nephites who had been visited by the Savior? We're told that "the Lord did prosper them exceedingly in the land; yea, insomuch that they did build cities again where there had been cities burned" (4 Nephi 1:7).

Planting and harvesting crops requires hard work. So does raising animals and rebuilding cities that have burned to the ground.

There you have it: two more embedded messages that teach us how to obtain happiness.

Wait, you are thinking. *Work is where happiness goes to die.* Not so! We need work if we want to be happy.

It's not just about being happy, either—it's part of God's plan for us. Did you ever consider the fact that God left the world unfinished so we could apply our skill and workmanship to it? That's what President Thomas S. Monson taught: "He left the electricity in the cloud, the oil in the earth. He left the rivers unbridged and the forests unfelled and the cities unbuilt. God gives to man the challenge of raw materials, not the ease of finished things. He leaves the pictures unpainted and the music unsung and the problems unsolved, that man might know the joys and glories of creation."[6] The Lord designed a classroom in which we would have to work hard.

Work and happiness go hand in hand. That's because the exhilaration of being creative and the boost of confidence that come along with hard work make us happy. Compare the feeling of accomplishment after a hard day's work to the feeling you have when you sleep in and don't do anything all day. Which one made you truly happier?

> We need work if we want to be happy. Did you ever consider the fact that God left the world unfinished so we could apply our skill and workmanship to it?

There's another important thing work does for us, and I can best illustrate that in an experience I had with one of my children. In our house, we like to raise chickens—not because I love chickens, but because I want my children to deal with death early on. I know it sounds morbid, but here's the way I figure it: if my children's first experiences dealing with death involve *chickens*, for crying out loud, then it's not going to be quite as traumatic for them when someone really close to them dies. (Someone closer than a chicken, I mean, like a grandparent or a friend. Does a chicken even count as a someone?) If you are going to have livestock, you'll eventually have deadstock. I don't think death will ever become an easy part of life, but I think by experiencing death on a smaller scale, they will be more apt to

6 "In Quest of the Abundant Life," *Ensign*, March 1988, 2.

take on the difficult challenge of losing a close friend or family member to death. I'm not basing this on any research that I know of, it just seems like good parenting to me.

It's not all about death and mourning. I guess the chickens provide some element of fun, too. At least the kids seem to think so.

One of my sons, Mason, is the most sensitive kid I've ever encountered. He *hates* to see anything—a brother, a pet, an insect—struggle or suffer. When we saw *Honey, I Shrunk the Kids*—if you haven't seen it, ask your mom about it—and the big ant got killed, Mason bawled his eyes out. I kinda stared at him trying desperately not to laugh. He definitely didn't get that from me. I'm not a fan of suffering, but the ant's sudden demise didn't even give me pause, let alone rock me to the core.

Now that you have some context about the chickens and about Mason, let's get on with the story. We carefully put a bunch of fertilized eggs in the incubator, and the kids spent the next twenty-eight days keeping a careful watch on our new chickens-to-be. Finally, there it was: music to our ears—the faint chirping sounds accompanied by little beaks trying to peck out of those eggs.

At that point, Mason tried to lift the lid off the incubator so he could help the little chickens escape by breaking their shells for them. And I—the big, mean dad—stopped him. I put the lid back on the incubator and told him that under no circumstance could he touch those eggs.

"You're mean!" he pouted.

"No, I'm not mean."

"Just listen to them! You're mean! I want to help them!" His sadness was turning to anger. I had the power to help them, and I wouldn't. He saw this as unfair and cruel.

And that's when I had to break the bad news to Mason: the struggle they were waging against that eggshell was going to give them strong wings and strong legs. Chickens with strong wings and legs are able to stand up and move. Chickens without strong legs fall over. Chickens who fall over can't eat. They die.

It was a tough lesson for Mason to learn, but he is a teachable kid (that's something he definitely got from me), and he finally said, "So their problems are actually *good* for them?"

"Yes," I replied, "If we helped them, we'd actually be hurting them." And at that point, Mason agreed with me that the best thing we could do was stand back and cheer them on.

And that's how it is in life. The Lord doesn't usually take away hard work, or problems, or trials, or even tragedy—even when we beg Him to intervene. But He does cheer us on.

The Lord doesn't usually take away hard work, or problems, or even tragedy—even when we beg Him to. But He does cheer us on.

Share What You Have

And now for another embedded message about happiness: Of that group of Nephites who were happier than any people ever created, Mormon wrote that they had "all things common among them" and that "there were not rich and poor" (4 Nephi 1:3).

In other words, if you want to be happy, share what you have with others.

That same message rings out loud and clear elsewhere in the Book of Mormon. As just one example, King Benjamin told his people, "I would that ye should impart of your substance to the poor, every man according to that which he hath, such as feeding the hungry, clothing the naked, visiting the sick, and administering to their relief, both spiritually and temporally, according to their wants" (Mosiah 4:26).

And it's not just the Book of Mormon—or any of the other scriptures, for that matter. In fact, many studies have shown that money spent on others and time spent serving them have a direct impact on our happiness.[7] Maybe that's one reason the Church offers

[7] See, for example, Dunn et al., "Spending Money on Others Promotes Happiness," *Science, 319* (2008), 1687–1688; Netta Weinstein and Richard M. Ryan, "When Helping Helps: Autonomous Motivation for Prosocial Behavior and Its Influence on Well-Being for the Helper and Recipient," *Journal of Personality and Social Psychology, 98* (2010), 222–224; and Aknin et al., "Pro-

so many service opportunities and chances to donate money (such as fast offerings and humanitarian projects). As we provide more of our time, means, and effort to others, our own happiness will grow.

There's more involved than our endeavors to boost our happiness. The mandate to help is an actual invitation from the Lord. In his October 2014 general conference address, Elder Jeffrey R. Holland said, "Down through history, poverty has been one of humankind's greatest and most widespread challenges. Its obvious toll is usually physical, but the spiritual and emotional damage it can bring may be even more debilitating. In any case, the great Redeemer has issued no more persistent call than for us to join Him in lifting this burden from the people."

Create Safety

Now that Nephi had his society up and running, and they were harvesting crops and working with ores and raising animals, he did something else that gives us a great embedded message about happiness. Nephi tells us that he "did take the sword of Laban, and after the manner of it did make many swords, lest by any means the people who were now called Lamanites should come upon us and destroy us" (2 Nephi 5:14).

Before you think I've lost *all* my marbles and am suggesting you stockpile a bunch of weapons if you want to be happy, consider what this embedded message *really* means: that if you want to feel happy, you need to feel safe and secure.

Here's an eye-opener from a different chapter that provides another embedded message on the same subject: Moroni tells us that "there never was a happier time among the people of Nephi, since the days of Nephi, than in the days of Moroni, yea, even at this time" (Alma 50:23). If you're familiar with the Book of Mormon, you know that "even at this time" was *smack dab* in the middle of a ferocious twenty-year war. How on earth could these people be so happy when there was a vicious war raging all around them? (And don't forget that the wars in the Book of Mormon were messy—the hand-to-

---

social Spending and Well-Being: Cross-Cultural Evidence for a Psychological Universal," *Journal of Personality and Social Psychology, 104* (2013), 635–652.

hand-combat, piling-up-of-bodies, swearing-to-drink blood sort of messy.) What's the embedded message for us?

Study those war chapters, and you'll find out what Moroni did—what he wants us to do: *prepare*. Moroni was *always* preparing for the future. You've read it before: those who are prepared don't feel afraid (see D&C 38:30). And people who aren't afraid feel safe. And you can figure out the rest: people who feel safe are happy.

Let me take a quick commercial break to mention one other thing: at the end of that twenty-year war, the people were divided into two camps. I'm not talking Nephite and Lamanite. I'm talking people who had been hardened by this very difficult experience and those who had become softened by it (check out Alma 62:41). That war—just like every other war, including the war against evil—became a divider. And that's still happening. And it's up to you whether you will be hardened or softened by any trial you face. Mormon leaves it up to you, but his embedded message is very clear about one thing: You have a choice. And you can choose happiness, even in difficult circumstances.

Back to our regular programming: in order to be happy, you need to feel safe—emotionally, physically, spiritually, mentally, financially. That means you need to try to surround yourself with people who prepare for the future and who provide safety in an environment that is safe. It's tough to be happy when you don't know if your spouse is going to be faithful or if you are up to your neck in debt. As you reduce the unpredictability and vulnerability in life, peace and happiness are allowed to flourish.

It also means you need to do your part in creating a safe environment for others. Conduct yourself so that others feel safe around you. They need to know what to expect from you. They need to know you are predictable—be the "Old Faithful" of your house (I guess you don't have to be old; be the "Young Faithful," for all I care). Create a home where everyone can have a sense of safety and security.

You're Invited to Be Happy

I've covered only some of the embedded messages these two chapters offer on how to achieve happiness. Now it's your turn: Read carefully, deeply, and look for what else is there. Then expand your search and look at the *rest* of the Book of Mormon. Remember, just because you don't see the principles at first, doesn't mean they aren't there. You have to think and reread—you have to dig.

The invitation to be happy was issued near the very beginning of the Book of Mormon when Lehi described his dream. He described the tree of life, "whose fruit was desirable to make one happy" (1 Nephi 8:10). In fact, he says that when he partook of the fruit, "it filled my soul with exceedingly great joy" (1 Nephi 8:12)—so much that he wanted his entire family to partake of it as well.

You, through a desperately long but very certain genealogy, are part of Lehi's family. He wants you—*you*—to partake of the fruit that will fill your soul with the greatest joy. What is the fruit? That fruit is the love of the Son of God, and the wisest souls recognize that happiness comes only through Jesus Christ, the Savior and Redeemer and the principles He taught and still teaches today. Develop a relationship with Him and your life will take on new meaning.

CHAPTER THREE

Learning to "Accentuate the Positive"

You probably think that optimism—as the dictionary defines it, the tendency to look on the more favorable side of events or conditions, the belief that goodness pervades reality—is a good thing. It is. Of course, there needs to be balance in everything, but generally speaking, having a positive outlook is a mighty healthy thing. And it absolutely leads to happiness.

But believe it or not, there's a lot of pressure in society to choose the opposite.

There are a lot of people who treat optimism like it's a negative thing, even a weakness. They will tell you that if you're an optimist you're not being realistic, skipping around in a pair of rose-tinted glasses that prevent you from seeing things as they really are. They tell you that if you don't see pain and ugliness or experience negative emotions, you're not mature or experienced in "real" life. They tell you that if you're a positive person, you're nuts; in essence, you're just lying to yourself. They'll even say that if you have positive expectations, you're more likely to take stupid risks or make unsound decisions.

That's because there are a *lot* of people who simply think that this world is a pretty negative place. They're convinced that things are bad and they are not going to get better. And if you don't agree with them, you're just not getting it. You need to grow up, they'll say.

It's simply not true. My differing is based on a lifetime of personal experience and hundreds of studies that say otherwise. It's also based on listening to the counsel of prophets and Apostles. One of the very best when it came to a positive outlook was President Gordon B. Hinckley.

Now don't go thinking that just because President Hinckley was the prophet, he had an easy life. Far from it. He had some pretty dire health problems. When he was just two, he got whooping cough—and it took forever for him to recover because of all the smoke from the coal-burning stoves in Salt Lake City. Then he developed serious allergies and earaches. As a result, the family built a summer home in East Millcreek Canyon and moved there for four months every year to get young Gordon out of the smoke and other gunk.

He also grew up in the bottom of the Great Depression, a time when Americans had to stand in long lines for hours just to buy bread. A time when you were lucky to have more than one pair of shoes or three meals a day.

When Gordon was twenty years old, his beloved mother passed away. "I recall the gray November day of her funeral," he later said. "We put on a front of bravery and fought back the tears, but inside, the wounds were deep and painful."

Then there was his mission. As soon as he stepped off the boat in England, he began weeping—not for joy and not out of homesickness, but from epic hay fever. After fighting his health and the Brits' lack of interest in the Church for as long as he could stand it, he wrote a discouraging letter home: he felt he was wasting his own time and his father's money.

You probably know his father's famous reply: "Forget yourself and go to work."

For the rest of his life, President Hinckley gave his days, months, and years to the Church. He was a counselor to three Presidents of the Church. He often had to carry the burden on his own when illness prevented other members of the First Presidency from work. He was often in his office by five a.m. and stayed until after dark—not just for years . . . for decades.

Knowing that President Hinckley's life was filled with plenty of trials makes it all the more amazing that he challenged us—in word and example—to have a more positive outlook. In a speech at Brigham Young University on October 29, 1974, he said, "I come this morning with a plea that we stop seeking out the storms and enjoy more fully the sunlight. I am suggesting that we 'accentuate the positive.' I am asking that we look a little deeper for the good, that we still our voices of insult and sarcasm, that we more generously compliment virtue and effort. . . .

"What I am suggesting and asking is that we turn from the negativism that so permeates our society and look for the remarkable good in the land and times in which we live, that we speak of one another's virtues more than we speak of one another's faults, that optimism replace pessimism, that our faith exceed our fears."

There you have it, straight from a prophet of God.

There's no immaturity there. He's not saying society is free of problems; he's saying we should look for the good. Because the good is there.

He not saying people don't have faults. He's saying just don't look for those faults. Focus on the good things.

He's asking that we replace pessimism with optimism—that our faith exceeds our fears.

President Hinckley asked that we replace pessimism with optimism—that our faith exceeds our fears.

It's fun to know, by the way, that President Hinckley had a wife who felt much the same way. She had to be so fun to live with! She wrote, "The only way to get through life is to laugh your way through it. You either have to laugh or cry. I prefer to laugh. Crying gives me a headache."[8]

It's also fun to know that scientific research backs up what President Hinckley said. Researcher Martin Seligman—a guy we've already talked about in this book—is the father of a movement called positive psychology. He's proven that you can actually change your outlook on life.

That's a revolutionary concept. Because before Dr. Seligman came along, the experts looked at things a whole lot differently. They

[8] Marjorie Pay Hinckley, *Small and Simple Things* [Salt Lake City: Deseret Book, 2003], 126.

maintained that you could *never* change the way you look at things. Oh, you could *pretend* to, they said, but you could never actually change. If you were born with a negative outlook, you would always have a negative outlook, no matter what. But then Seligman started using positive psychology and *proved*—with controlled studies and neuroimaging—you *can* rewire your brain.

Think about that for just a minute. That goes along perfectly with what the gospel teaches. We are asked to repent—to put off the natural man and become a Saint (see Mosiah 3:19). The only way we can do that is by changing. And the Lord understood that such change was possible *long* before Dr. Seligman and positive psychology came along.

We looked at the scriptures a bit in the last chapter, and I want to do that again—because Nephi and his brothers once again provide a perfect example, this time of outlook on life. You already know that Lehi and his family fled Jerusalem and beat a rugged path through a heartless wilderness in their search for the promised land. Nephi was there; so was his brother Laman. They had the exact same experiences, but they definitely didn't see them the same way.

Here's Nephi's summation of the events:

"And so great were the blessings of the Lord upon us, that while we did live upon raw meat in the wilderness, our women did give plenty of suck for their children, and were strong, yea, even like unto the men; and they began to bear their journeyings without murmurings.

"And thus we see that the commandments of God must be fulfilled. And if it so be that the children of men keep the commandments of God he doth nourish them, and strengthen them, and provide means whereby they can accomplish the thing which he has commanded them; wherefore, he did provide means for us while we did sojourn in the wilderness" (1 Nephi 17:2–3).

Nephi must have had some seriously strong neurotransmitters. How does life in the wilderness sound according to him? Pretty amazing, right? He's making it sound like one of the best experiences of his life.

Do you really think Nephi believed all those things he was saying? Or do you just think he was trying to convince himself? Those are interesting questions, and we'll talk about them more in a minute.

But first, let's look at how Laman sized up the whole wilderness experience:

"[Our father] hath led us out of the land of Jerusalem, and we have wandered in the wilderness for these many years; and our women have toiled, being big with child; and they have borne children in the wilderness and suffered all things [maybe they're talking about the raw meat], save it were death; and it would have been better that they had died before they came out of Jerusalem than to have suffered these afflictions [nice thing to say to your wife: you'd be better off dead].

"Behold, these many years we have suffered in the wilderness, which time we might have enjoyed our possessions and the land of our inheritance; yea, and we might have been happy" (1 Nephi 17:20–21).

Wait, didn't Nephi and Laman have the same experiences?

Yes. Yes, they did.

But they definitely didn't describe those experiences the same way.

No. No, they didn't.

That's because they didn't experience them in the same way at all.

In the last chapter, we talked about embedded messages. What is the Lord trying to teach us? Well there's a big principle here, and you can see it in the last five words of Laman: WE MIGHT HAVE BEEN HAPPY. You don't want to be like Laman, because for Laman, happiness was always someplace else.

> Laman said, "*We might have been happy. . . .*" You don't want to be like Laman, because for Laman, happiness was always someplace else.

Check it out. I'd be happy *if* we were back home in Jerusalem with all the wealth and land. Next, I'd be happy *if* Nephi hadn't broken his bow. Then, I'd be happy if we were just off this miserable boat. Then, I'd be happy *if* I was just away from Nephi. Finally, I'd be happy *if* Nephi was dead. And on and on it goes. I'd be happy *if*. . .

Nobody wants to be like Laman, but how many times have we thought those same sorts of things? Have you ever thought or said, "If things were different, then I would be happy"? This sort of trap can actually start early in life. If I was just bigger, I'd be happier. If I was just sixteen and I could drive and date, I'd be happier. If I could just graduate from high school, I'd be happier. If I could just get my own car and move out of this house, I'd be happier. If I was only married, I would be happier. If I could just lose some weight, I'd be happier. If only I had kids, I'd be happier. If I didn't have this calling, I'd be happier. If only I had a better job, I'd be happier. If the kids would just leave, I'd be happier. If I could only retire, I'd be happier. One day my grandma actually said to me, "Hank, if I was dead, I think I'd be happier."

Does it ever stop? I don't think so, because I'm convinced there are people in the spirit world who are saying, "If I was just resurrected, I'd be happier."

It's a big problem, this "if things were different, then I'd be happy" complex. Laman had it bad. After rehearsing all his complaints, remember, he wished things had been different and ended with, "We might have been happy."

The "If things were different, I'd be happy" myth has a friend. I call it the "myth of future me." You know:

The future me is gonna be different.

The future me is gonna lose some weight.

The future me is gonna eat better.

The future me is gonna be a better parent.

The future me is gonna be a lot happier.

The today me? Not so much. But the future me is going to be *way better.*

Then, ten years down the road (or a few weeks before a high school reunion) you suddenly wake up and think, *Hey, the future should be here by now.* And it occurs to you that the future me is a little late showing up on the scene. So what do we do next is go back to the "If things were different, then I would be happy" myth for comfort. These two myths perpetuate and deceptively reassure each other. "Someday," we say to pacify ourselves, "when things are different and future me is here, then I'll be happy." Without an incentive, like that high school reunion or the knowledge that you are going to be in a public place in a swimming suit, these two myths pat you on the head, give you a pacifier, and sing you to sleep.

Well, it's time to wake up. Here's the truth: there is no "future me." There's only "today me." Because if you're not willing to do something today, you'll never do it tomorrow. If you're not going to give up Diet Coke (or whatever resolution you have) today, you're not going to give it up tomorrow. Nope, you're going to die with a can of Diet Coke in your hand. The "future me" is going to be no different than the "today me," except just a little more used to things. If you aren't willing to do something for the rest of your life, why are you doing it today?

Here's a second dish of truth. If things were different, you wouldn't be happier, you'd be the exact same. We've already discussed this at length, so I won't go over it again. Circumstances rarely determine happiness. We think they do, but they don't. If things were different . . . your happiness level would be the exact same. Laman was stuck in the cyclical nature of these two myths. Are you?

So let's go back to Nephi. I asked if you thought he really believed what he wrote or if he was just trying to convince himself. Well, I think he really believed it. Here's why: First, Nephi didn't always feel this way about his father's ideas. He wrote in 1 Nephi 2:16 that the Lord softened his heart so he could believe in the words of his father. Your heart only needs to be softened if it is hardened.

Second, after his heart is softened, he never makes himself look like a hero for seeing the wilderness as a positive experience. He never says, "This was awful, but look at how positive I'm being!" Nephi isn't a martyr. He seems to have trained himself to accentuate the positive. Where's happiness for Nephi? "Everywhere!" he would tell us. He scarcely had to look an inch to find it. *Raw meat?* Love it! *My wife is like a man?* Love that too! *Wilderness?* Love it! It's the best! I've found some great things out here in the wilderness! I've learned so much about myself, the Lord, and our relationship!

Really? Yes, really. Because Nephi somehow changed his mindset. Through the Spirit he seems to have engrained this truth into his character: circumstance really has very little influence on happiness. Happiness is a result of a particular mindset, a choice that flows from character. (When I say that, I see an exception for those with depression; more about that later.)

Elder Jeffrey R. Holland has a firm understanding of that. In his April 2007 general conference address, he said, "Yes, life has its problems, and yes, there are negative things to face, but please accept one of Elder Holland's maxims for living—no misfortune is so bad that whining about it won't make it worse." In that same talk, in fact, he mentioned Nephi, supposing that the beatings from his brothers must surely have been easier to take than their constant murmuring: "Surely [Nephi] must have said at least once, 'Hit me one more time. I can still hear you.'"

> **Happiness results from a particular mindset. It is a choice that flows from character.**

We've been taught that we all have spiritual gifts. I believe *anyone* can learn to have a more positive outlook, but I think it's also possible for people to be born with the gift of being optimistic, of seeing things through a positive lens. Others of us get to develop that gift as we go along.

Take a look at Thomas Edison. He was naturally very optimistic, which might be one of the reasons he was so successful. (You may not realize it, but he still holds the record for the most patents filed with the U.S. Patent Office. All these years later.)

When he was just twelve years old, Edison lost most of his hearing. His parents were devastated. I think most parents would be devastated facing a situation like that. But Edison himself was just fine. He told his parents he kind of liked it—he said it helped him concentrate.

By the time he was in his thirties, he had made fourteen hundred prototypes for a lightbulb that could be used by the general public. I don't know if you're aware of this, but a prototype is no walk in the park—you have to design a product, then make it, then test it. And none of Edison's prototypes worked. The newspapers had a heyday; the headlines read, "Edison fails to make the lightbulb."

Wait until you read how Edison, the optimist, answered: "I have not failed. I have found 1,400 ways in which it won't work." He saw each "failure" as one more step forward. One more discovery. One more way to get closer and closer to his goal.

As if that wasn't enough, fast-forward to December 9, 1914: An explosion in Edison's film inspection building caused a fire that destroyed more than half of the buildings in his laboratory. The fire caused $7 million in damages to structures that were painfully underinsured—not to mention destroying a large amount of his work. He was sixty-seven, not exactly the age you want to be when you are forced to start over.

Imagine how you'd feel in that situation. Years of work burning in flames. Now check out what happened next. Edison's son arrived at the scene to see the firefighters standing helplessly, just staring at the horrific blaze, which was too out of control to even fight. Edison himself stood next to them, his white hair blowing in the wind and his face glowing with the reflection of the flames. As soon as Edison saw his son, he turned to him and shouted, "Go find your mother. She'll never see a fire like this as long as she lives."

Asked by bystanders what he was going to do in the face of such devastation, Edison vowed, "I'll start all over again tomorrow."

And he did.

The next day, all seven thousand employees reported for duty. And as they gathered around Edison, he said something that some would consider borderline delusional: "There is great value in this disaster, my friends. All of our mistakes are burned up. Thank heaven we can start anew." All of the mistakes are burned up? Was he serious?

I'm convinced Edison was born with a gift for positivity—but I'm just as convinced that those who aren't can train their brains to accentuate the positive, which leads to greater happiness. I'm going to share with you now one of my prouder moments, a time when I actually practiced what I teach.

Okay, my experience wasn't quite as expensive as Edison's towering laboratory fire, but at the time it might have felt just as harrowing. Unbeknownst to us, our sprinkler pipe broke early one afternoon and starting filling the window well with water. When the window well was about three-fourths full, the pressure exerted by the water caused the window to break. And you know where all that water went. That's right: into the basement.

By the time I realized there was a problem and scuttled down to the basement, there was a good four or five inches of water throughout the entire thing. Water. I'm sure my eyes got wide and my face got really red as one word kept pounding through my head: *Expensive, expensive, expensive, expensive.* Somewhere in the distant catacombs of my brain I could hear various voices shouting "Oh no no no no no no." I saw thousand-dollar bills with legs and arms waving good-bye to me as they ran and jumped down the toilet. Luckily, I had enough wits about me to get the power turned off to the basement so we would all be safe.

Then the silence fell like a pall over the place. I was standing there, probably still wide-eyed and red-faced, and my kids were standing there staring at me. For the briefest moment, there was an impasse—Dad paralyzed by images of costly repairs, kids paralyzed by thoughts of what Dad might do next. I could just hear what they were thinking: *Oh no. Dad's going to freak out BIG-TIME. Run, guys, he's gonna blow!*

"Get your swimsuits on! How often do you get a chance to swim in the basement?"

But I didn't. My study of President Hinckley, Nephi, and Thomas Edison paid off. I was mindful enough to realize this was an opportunity to forge my character. I took a deep breath, smiled, and said, "Get your swimsuits on! How often do you get a chance to swim in the basement?" And that's exactly what we did. We swam in the basement. We played and ran and slid around on the carpet. I could have looked at that very expensive problem and sized up everything that was wrong with it, but instead I looked for what was right. And I'm happy to report that we made some fun memories that night, swimming in the basement. Didn't even have to worry about sunscreen. And yes, in case you were wondering, it was expensive to repair. However, I'm absolutely certain it would have been just as expensive if I had become angry and lost my temper in front of my children. I wasn't naturally accentuating the positive yet, but I was one step closer to it.

Developing the Gift

All of this boils down to how we think about our situation and whatever is happening to us. So who controls that? We do. How can you develop this gift to accentuate the positive? Keep reading.

First, you need to understand the nature of anticipation. You've undoubtedly experienced this yourself. Let's say you're planning a family trip to Disneyland. The anticipation is incredible. Bring on the rapture! Your neurotransmitters are pumping out happiness like candy on Halloween. You're going to do this and that and go here and there and *no one* forget to ride Pirates of the Caribbean! You even detect a taste of a Disneyland turkey leg in your mouth. Your brain is practically there.

Then you get to Disneyland. It's three-thirty in the afternoon and the lines are obscenely long and you haven't ridden half the rides you wanted to and the kids are tired and grumpy and everyone's fighting about what to do next and no one wants to eat the picnic lunch you packed—they all want overpriced corn dogs. And now *you're* the bad guy because you paid a month's salary to get park-hopper passes for everyone and EVERYONE IS GOING TO STAY UNTIL MIDNIGHT AND BE HAPPY—EVEN IF IT KILLS THEM.

What happened to all that cheerful anticipation? Face it. Anticipation doesn't include the long lines and sunburned necks and whining toddlers and blistered feet. It doesn't even start to account for the lost diaper bag or the sudden (but thankfully brief) rainstorm or the kids with motion sickness from the newest ride. Nope. None of that stuff got any air time at all. Anticipation and reality can be two vastly different experiences.

So if you want to be happy, you should just anticipate but never actually *do* anything? No, that's not what I'm saying at all. What I'm saying is this: you need to achieve balance. There's a human tendency to exaggerate in our anticipation. Ever dreaded a dentist visit for days only to walk out thinking, *That wasn't so bad*? Then you know what I'm talking about. We anticipate bad things will be way worse than they actually are and we anticipate good things will be too incredible for words. Neither of which usually ends up being true. It's wise to watch out for this tendency. It's okay to be nervous about a potentially negative event, but don't let that paralyze you; it likely isn't going to be as bad as you think. It's also okay to be excited for a potentially fun event, just don't let that lead to frustration and disappointment if it doesn't turn out exactly the way you had envisioned.

Understanding how the brain anticipates both potentially good and potentially bad future events is crucial to developing the gift of positivity. Instead of being a victim to anticipation and disappointment, you can control those emotions and take steps to train your brain to look for the good in any situation.

What do I mean by not being a victim of anticipation? Everyone has problems. There are negative elements in every life. You can't wish them away or ignore them. That's scary in a whole new way. Someone who anticipates *only the good* is often completely blindsided when the first hard, cannot-ignore problem comes along; he's done for because he doesn't have any experience in confronting problems. A problem is a complete threat to his carefully constructed, perfect plan. His anticipation has caused him to live life with his eyes closed, and now he's going to pay for it.

Anticipating that problems will need to be faced and will need to be solved is vital to happiness. But make no mistake about it—you can face and tackle your problems with a positive mindset, and chances are you'll be a lot happier along the way.

What do I mean about not being a victim to disappointment? The other side of the spectrum is the person who anticipates only the negative because they've experienced so much disappointment. Cynicism has become a guiding philosophy in life. There are a number of examples I can think of. A new missionary arrives in the mission field, expressing the desire to change lives. A worn-out old elder ready to step on the plane home scoffs at him and says, "You ain't changing *anybody's* life." A couple gets engaged and some well-meaning bundle of joy says, "Oh, hope you've had fun, because *that's* over. Marriage is the absolute hardest thing!" A couple decides to have children, and the same friends have a new refrain: "Well, hope you've had a good life. Call me when they're eighteen and we can pick back up." We've all met these type of folks.

Do those sound like the words of happy people? There is no joy in living that way. They take all the excitement out of good news.

Anticipating that life will deal you the worst every single day doesn't make you more mature or more realistic, it just makes you no fun to be around.

On one side of the spectrum you live with your eyes closed. On the other side—the cynical side—of the spectrum are those who live with their hearts closed.

But can you live with your eyes wide open *and* your heart wide open as well?

Your eyes need to be wide open enough to anticipate that life will have real difficulties—that difficulties are unavoidable. However, your heart needs to be wide open enough to rely on the Lord to help you solve them—to have the trust and the faith to know that disappointment is an important part of this mortal classroom and that you will come through any difficulty stronger than you were when you went in. That mindset is at the heart of accentuating the positive.

> Your eyes need to be wide open enough to anticipate that life will have real difficulties—but your heart needs to be wide open enough to rely on the Lord to help you solve them.

Second, now that you understand the nature of anticipation, you must do something that trains your brain to naturally look for the positive and focus on it. Here's an idea that research has shown to be very effective: a gratitude journal.

I can almost hear the moaning and groaning now. *A journal?* Maybe you've tried that before, and you bailed pretty quickly because it was a drag. Took too much time. Or maybe you've never even tried it before because you knew right off that it was going to take too much energy.

Well, you're right. Keeping a journal *does* take energy. But here's the good part: a gratitude journal doesn't take the same kind of energy as a here's-what-happened-today journal or a here-are-my-existential-thoughts-on-world-conditions type of journal. *This* kind of journal is not that involved, and it's one of the most sure-fire ways to change your outlook and bring you happiness for what ends up being a minimal investment.

Here's what you do. Get something to use as your journal. If you want, you can buy a nice journal or a beautiful hardbound notebook; if not, you can use something a lot less formal. Now, every night, write down three things for which you were grateful that day. The three things have to be things that were specific to *that day*. No repeats—that's cheating! But stick with it. Do it every single day for thirty days.

Participants in gratitude journal research have seen some amazing things happen. First off, they find themselves actually *looking for* things that bring them gratitude and happiness. They have begun to train their brain to see the good in each day. But even more incredible, they have started seeing circumstances they would have normally described as negative in a positive light.

A friend of mine found her mother's gratitude journal a few days after her mother's death. One of the entries illustrates exactly what I mean here. The woman's cat had fallen ill and needed to be taken to the vet. This woman could have complained about the hassle of having to take the cat to the vet. Or she very justifiably could have whined about the expensive vet bill. She even could have carped about the fact that her pet should have been listed as a dependent on her health insurance. Nope. Not our gratitude journal woman. Pen in hand, she expressed gratitude that she had enough money to pay the vet so her cat could be treated and the animal's pain relieved.

Write just three things a day, and you will train your brain to see the positive in each day. Your brain will then start to emphasize the positive without you having to give it a conscious thought. Before long, you will find yourself focusing on the good things in your day. You will be happier. Science backs that up, and the changes you experience will become permanent. How could that possibly not be worth a few minutes a day?

And another thing will likely happen: if you make it through the first thirty days, you will probably keep going. Sure, it will still take some energy, but you'll find you enjoy it. Maybe even get a kick out of it. And like the woman who had enough money to take her cat to the vet, you might actually keep doing it for years. And when *you* die, your son or daughter might find all those volumes and find a reason to be happy too.

A second idea to help you learn to accentuate the positive is easier, and it takes only *two minutes*. I don't care how busy you are or how overscheduled your day is, you can spare *two minutes*. Here's how it works: for two full minutes (and it has to be two full minutes at a time, three or four or five would be even better), focus your mind on a specific happy thought. It doesn't matter what it is. It could be something as simple as the time your son tackled an opponent so hard you feared he had eviscerated the kid—then your son reached down, helped the boy up, and put his arm around him as they both walked toward the sidelines. Or how about the time your daughter fished frantically through her trick-or-treat bag, finally found her favorite treat, and offered it to you. Or maybe the time you just sat and rocked your newborn granddaughter to sleep. Or the time you saw a sunset that absolutely took your breath away. Mine would have something to do with my wife and children—a memory of spending time with them.

Science has proven that if you spend two full minutes focused on a happy thought, *your brain actually starts making you happier.*

Here's what happens: science has proven that if you will spend two full minutes focused on a happy thought, *your brain actually starts making you happier*. You can convince your brain that you are happy. That's right. You have the power to physically change your brain. So do it, every day. Consider it your happiness workout. In fact, whenever you start feeling the desire to be just a little happier, go to your happy place. Spend two full minutes there. I promise it works.

Why go through all of this work and effort just to simply learn how to accentuate the positive? What if I told you it might just save your life? What if I told you it will help you manage grief and survive the most difficult of circumstances? So you can better understand what I mean, I have two real-life examples of exactly what I'm talking about.

Happiness Stronger than Pain

Let's start with Admiral Jim Stockdale—full name, believe it or not, James Bond Stockdale. You've got to love that. A United States Navy vice admiral, he was leading aerial attacks from the *U.S.S. Ticonderoga* during the 1964 Gulf of Tonkin incident. (Actually, "incident" doesn't even start to do this maelstrom justice.) Happy day, he survived that.

But it's hard to keep a good man down, so Stockdale went on to another deployment. He wasn't so lucky that time: he was shot down over North Vietnam on September 9, 1965. His plane, a Douglas A-4 Skyhawk, was struck by enemy fire and completely disabled. Stockdale ejected from his plane, breaking a bone in his back, and parachuted into a small village. There he was captured by what he describes as a "thundering herd" bent on protecting their village—"the quarterback sack of the century," he called it. They tore off his clothes and severely beat him, breaking his leg and paralyzing his arm. He was then taken as a prisoner of war to Hoa Lo Prison. You might know it as the infamous "Hanoi Hilton."

The Hanoi Hilton was no laughing matter. North Vietnam had signed the Third Geneva Convention of 1949, which demanded "decent and humane treatment" of prisoners of war, but you'd never know it. They used the most severe torture tactics, including beatings, irons, rope bindings, and prolonged solitary confinement. Stockdale was the highest-ranking military officer at the Hanoi Hilton, where he was a prisoner of war for eight years. Let that sink in before you move on—*eight years*. You've undoubtedly heard of one of his fellow prisoners: U.S. presidential candidate and Arizona Senator John McCain.

Stockdale paints a grim picture of his time at the Hilton. He was beaten unconscious sixteen or seventeen times. He was chained in heavy, abrasive leg irons for more than two years. He was left without food for days and was denied medical care. He was left in an isolated cell for more than two years, a period during which he never saw another American. Another time, he was kept in total darkness in solitary confinement for four years. For him, one of the worst offenses was being deprived receiving letters from home. Because worse than the pain and torture for Stockdale was not knowing whether he would ever see his family again. It is difficult for me to even *write* this description; he had to *live* it.

Here's the kind of grit this guy was made of. At one point, they actually stopped beating him. They started giving him food. He actually started looking a bit robust and healthy. And then he found out what they were up to: he was told that he was going to be taken "downtown" and paraded before a group of foreign journalists, used as proof that they were treating their prisoners well.

Stockdale was infuriated. He was *not* going to be used like that. So he took a razor and repeatedly slit his scalp, disfiguring himself. When his captors told him they would cover his scalp with a hat, he retaliated with the only weapon at his disposal: he used a three-legged stool, the only piece of furniture in his cell, to beat himself, breaking some bones in his face until he was no longer recognizable. He figured they would never display a prisoner who appeared to be beaten.

His bravado didn't end there. When he found out that some of his fellow prisoners were being tortured to death, he slit his wrists. His message? He would rather take his own life than submit to their torture.

Well, he made it, and he eventually came back home to his family. He was awarded the Medal of Honor, three Navy Distinguished Service Medals, two Purple Heart Medals, and a host of other decorations.

Here's the really interesting part—the stuff that's relevant to our discussion of optimism and pessimism. Stockdale was interviewed at length about what happened during his imprisonment.

He told the reporter, "The pessimists died first." Why? For them, it was over the minute they were captured. They couldn't even envision a scenario in which they could fight or even survive. They quickly broke down mentally and soon died.

No one was too surprised by that. But what he said next startled even the experts: the next ones to die were the optimists. *What?* The optimists? Here's how Stockdale explained it: "Oh, they were the ones who said, 'We're going to be out by Christmas.' And Christmas would come, and Christmas would go. Then they'd say, 'We're going to be out by Easter.' And Easter would come, and Easter would go. And then Thanksgiving, and then it would be Christmas again. And they died of a broken heart."[9] They were disappointed too many times.

Stockdale then added what I've been trying to say in this chapter: "This is a very important lesson. You must never confuse faith that you will prevail in the end—which you can never afford to lose—with the discipline to confront the most brutal facts of your current reality, whatever they might be."[10]

The ones who survived, then, were the ones who had their eyes *and* their hearts wide open. They faced their reality with eyes wide open, but they believed they could overcome no matter the cost—hearts wide open as well. For them, accentuating the positive was much deeper than putting on a happy face; it had become part of their character

To conclude, let me share a story from my own experience that literally changed my life. About nineteen years ago, I met just about the most positive person I've ever known. He's not the irritating type who says, "Hey, everything's the best—I have no problems!" Nope, he's the type who lights up a room when he walks in because he is so determined to look on the bright side, despite the problems. Behind his smile is a life that has known his fair share of difficulty.

You need some background here, or you won't get the magnitude of what happened. Rodney was born in Richfield, Utah, and grew up there in the 1950s. Everything there was black-and-white. I know because I've seen the pictures.

As he tells it, he used to spend a lot of time at the Richfield Dairy

---

[9] Joanne Kimberlin, "Our POWs: Locked Up for 6 Years, He Unlocked a Spirit Inside," *The Virginian Pilot*, November 11, 2008, 12–13.

[10] Ibid.

because that was the place in town where you could get penny candy. (You know, back in the day—the candy you could get five or six or seven pieces for a penny.) And whenever Rodney got a little too unruly, his dad told him to take his brother down to the dairy and buy some penny candy.

One day as they waited their turn to get penny candy, the bell on the door rang, and in walked a girl he had seen before but hadn't ever really noticed. Well, he noticed her this time, and from that minute on he was fascinated. When I asked if he was in love, he said, "Uh, no. I was nine."

Well, he may not have been in love, but he was definitely enchanted. He remembers feeling like it was the first time he'd ever really seen a girl. Apparently, she was *very* aware that he was looking at her—and she remained very proper and polite and quiet, unlike Rodney. She ordered her candy, thanked the cashier, and left. Well, it must have been a bit of a big deal, because when Rodney got in the car, his mom asked him about the girl he'd been "studying."

Fast-forward a few years. Rodney, now known as Rod, was in high school, and he still kept his eye on the girl from the dairy, Marlene Baker. He had never really talked to her. They didn't have the same group of friends. Hers were the ones who wanted to get good grades and have bright futures; his were the ones who viewed teachers as an obstacle to having fun. Rodney was the guy who wore the coconut bra in *South Pacific*. That should paint a pretty clear picture.

One day Rod was in the counselor's office when the counselor asked who he was going to take to the junior prom.

"I'm not taking anybody," Rod told him. "I don't go to those kinds of things."

The counselor's response stopped Rod cold: "That's too bad. I think every girl deserves to go to prom."

Rod had never thought of it that way. So he started thinking about it, and eventually decided he would ask Marlene. He'd never talked to her—but he was fascinated. Still. Clear back from that first day in the Richfield Dairy.

Well, this was back in the day when you didn't have to spend $5,000 to ask a girl to prom. All you had to do was call her up. So he called Marlene, identified himself, and asked her to go to prom.

She was speechless. He interpreted that as maybe her fascination with *him*. Nope. She was stunned to silence because she was trying to figure out who he was. But props to Marlene: she accepted the invitation and even said that would be fun. Then she spent the next few days continuing to try to figure out who he was.

Finally it hit her. She knew him: he was the class clown. She'd seen him on stage a few times. He was a real goof. She just never knew his *name*.

Well, according to Rod, something magical happened at that prom. He started thinking about his future. When Marlene asked where he was going to go to college, he was dumbstruck. He'd never even thought about it. But now he did. He'd never been on a date before in his life, but he had a glorious time.

Something magical happened for Marlene at that prom too. She had been raised in a not-so-happy family and had endured a very difficult childhood. That night at the prom, dancing with Rod, she laughed harder than she had ever laughed. It was as though the bluebird of happiness set up permanent residence on her shoulder.

You might guess what happened from there. They got married right out of high school. She was still pretty serious; he was still very playful. In fact, the first day of their honeymoon they played in the pool before going back to their room. Not long after, there was a knock on the door. When Marlene answered, the grinning little boy who led the pack asked, "Can your son come out and play?"

A few years later when they welcomed their first child, Rod was determined to give baby Justin a tour of the house. Over Marlene's protests that the baby was only two days old, Rod cradled Justin in his arms and showed him every single feature of their cramped two-bedroom apartment: every light switch, every pot and pan, the piano, the shower. "This is the family room, where you and I are going to watch John Wayne," he said. "And here's the cookie jar, where Mom is going to make sure that you and I always have cookies." On it went, until every square inch of the place had been discovered.

Okay, Justin slept through most of it. After all, he was two days old. But it was so fun that it became a family tradition. The second baby got a tour. The third baby got a tour. And so on through all the kids. I need to tell you that I married their fifth child—the only normal one. The others are great, but nothing compared to their sister.

Fast-forward a couple of decades, and Justin welcomed *his* first baby into the world. Rod and Marlene, now Grandpa and Grandma, were elated—time for the tours to start up again! They gathered all of us up—and by now it was quite the crowd—and off we went, looking at every little feature of the house. It was my first tour, and I was a bit baffled. By the time we got to the third showerhead, I looked at my wife out of the corner of my eye, and she whispered, "Just go with it. It's what we do."

Let me just tell you: all five of my kids have been on that tour. The twins got a "two-at-a-time" tour. They loved it. Rod is still pure fun, and we were all reaping the benefits of his positive personality.

Then on my daughter's ninth birthday, we were eating at a Mexican restaurant when we got the phone call that would change our lives: Marlene had been diagnosed with stage-four liver cancer. They gave her five months to live.

Marlene defied the odds and actually made it ten months. It was a difficult and tear-filled year. At the end, she was on hospice care at home, sitting in a wheelchair, when the hospice nurse whispered, "Rod, judging by Marlene's vital signs, she's going to pass away in the next hour or two. We need to help her get into bed."

But as they started wheeling the chair down the hall, Rod turned to his kids and tried to muster some of his trademark cheer. In quiet tears, he gently said, "Let's go on one more tour." With his children and some grandchildren reverently following, he slowly pushed the wheelchair and then stopped and knelt, gently touching Marlene's hand.

"Marlene, we're in the living room. Forty-seven years of family home evening; how did you do it? How on earth did you put up with these kids?" There were expressions of gratitude and a few memories shared.

He carefully wheeled the chair to the family room. Kneeling again in front of her, he said, "Marlene, how many television shows have we watched in here? How many Westerns did I make you sit through?"

Next he pushed her chair to the kitchen, knelt in front of her again, and kissed her on the cheek. "You were the best cook in the entire world." My wife, Sara, claimed she saw a smile on her mom's face as if she was laughing, *You liar.*

At that point, the kids hung back as Rod talked to his wife about each child and the investment she had made in each of them. They're not all perfect. Not all served missions. Not all got married in the temple. But they're all good people with kind hearts. And Marlene played no small part in that.

As the tour drew to a close, Rod picked up his bride of forty-seven years—that fascinating little girl in the Richfield Dairy with her little sack of penny candy—and gently put her down in the bed. There he knelt by her side for the next six hours until she drifted through the veil.

A few weeks later we were in the car—me, my rambunctious bunch, and my father-in-law. My boys were yelling from the back, "Grandpa! Grandpa! Grandpa!"

"Guys, how about we leave Grandpa alone? This really isn't a good time." But the eager shouts continued, so I finally threw my phone back there. They were on it like a school of piranhas. They forgot all about Grandpa.

I turned to him and asked, "Hey, how are you doing this?"

"How am I doing what?"

"Aren't you supposed to be curled up in the fetal position in a closet somewhere?"

"Maybe." At that point, the tears started slipping down his cheeks. "I'll be honest. I'm dying. I still reach for her hand at night. I still pick up the phone to text her when I leave the office. I still call her name. The other night I saw something really funny on TV, and I called out, 'Marlene, you've got to come and see this!'"

I silently watched the road ahead but could feel his daunting pain. Then, almost too quiet to hear, he drew his line in the sand, as if he was letting life know where he stood. "One: if I have to live without her for a few years to really appreciate her, I'm willing to do that. And two: Hank, I'm a positive person. That's not going to change."

That moment has been engraved in my heart and mind forever.

For him, and for all of us, American author Joseph Campbell summed it up nicely when he said, "Find a place inside where there's joy, and the joy will burn out the pain."

CHAPTER FOUR

I Want Patience—And I Want It *Now*!

Everyone knows this: if you want to shoot a gun, pull the trigger.

Not as many people know this: if you want to annihilate your happiness, pull the trigger.

It's not the same trigger, of course.

The trigger on a gun activates the mechanism that discharges the weapon. Put a little pressure on it, and *bang*! The gun fires.

In this chapter, we're going to be talking about a different kind of trigger. The kind that sets off a reaction or a series of reactions or even a chain of events. This kind of trigger fires *you*. When you respond to this trigger, you're no longer in charge of yourself. Instead of being in control, you're operating on autopilot. Patience, kindness, understanding—all of it goes out the window. And somewhere along the way, your happiness goes down in flames. And in the end, it can also cause damage that rivals the best gun out there. When selfishness, impatience, and anger take over, happiness dies a painful death.

> This kind of trigger fires *you*. Patience goes out the window, and your happiness goes down in flames.

Hold on. This sounds like a dreadful scenario—and maybe happiness is the least of the casualties. Not so much. Here's why: patience is radically important. Let's give a bow to the scientists again, because they've proven that patience is linked to happiness. In fact, patience is tied to all kinds of positive emotions. They've proven that patience is correlated with less depression. People who are patient are warmer and kinder. They experience less conflict. They get better grades in school; they're more goal oriented throughout their lives. They suffer fewer health problems. And this bears repetition: they are happier. After all, you're holding this book in your hands because you want to learn how to be a little happier yourself. Well, patience is a key.

You can rewire your brain so you become more patient.

That's all great if you're patient, right? So what if you're not patient? Can you change? Can you become more patient? Yes. You can rewire your brain so you become more patient. I'd like to show you how. And I want to warn you that it involves triggers—more commonly known in research as *stimuli.*

First, let me share one of the most beautiful examples of patience I've ever heard of. Elder Robert C. Oaks shared it in his general conference address in October 2006. He told of a young man—let's call him Nick, though Elder Oaks didn't—whose father owned a motorcycle dealership. One day Nick's dad received a shipment of shiny new motorcycles. The two of them carefully lined all the new bikes up across the showroom floor. It must have been a sweet sight.

Once his dad went to the back to do a bunch of paperwork, Nick did what any young man would do. After circling his prey for a minute, Nick climbed right up on the motorcycle at the head of the line. What a beauty! Trembling with anticipation, he even started it up and gave it a few good revs.

Figuring he'd pushed his luck as far as he could, he switched off the ignition and jumped down. Let's just say Nick's dismount was not the smoothest ever recorded. He stood there in shock as that shiny new motorcycle tipped over—hitting the one next to it. That one hit the one next to it and so on. I know you can see in your mind's eye all those bikes toppling like dominoes, clear down to the very last one. The smashing and crunching were probably deafening.

Nick's dad, hearing the commotion (how could he *not*?), stepped into the showroom just in time to see all those formerly shiny new motorcycles on the floor, pieces and parts creased and dented, a few tires slowly spinning. You've got to imagine that Nick was terrified, anticipating what his dad was about to do at any second.

Instead of erupting with rage, his dad demonstrated an almost supernatural display of parental patience. He calmly said with a hint of a smile, "Well, son, we'd better fix one up and sell it so we can pay for the rest of them."

Amazing.

Nick never forgot that as long as he lived. In fact, according to Elder Oaks, he related it at his father's funeral.

Maybe you've had times like that—times when you were an absolute beacon of patience. Maybe you've practically brought home Olympic gold in the patience triathlon. Maybe there were other times when you didn't do so well—or times when you flat-out bit the dust in the patience arena. A lot of how you do when it comes to patience involves those blasted triggers. Respond to them, and your patience flees like Joseph from Potiphar's wife. Ignore them, and you can choose to come off like Nick's dad in the motorcycle melee. In fact, your chosen response to those triggers holds the key as to whether you can change—can become a more patient person. And if you can become more patient, you will likely become happier. Simple as that.

To understand the power of stimulus, you need to understand more of how the brain works. Don't panic. It's easy: stimulus > behavior > reward. It's actually a pretty primitive chain of events. A stimulus fires, it prompts a behavior, and you get a reward. I can give you a simple example from my own life that has happened too many times to count. Stimulus: Diet Coke sign or even a Diet Coke thought. Behavior: I buy one. Reward: I drink it. Rinse and repeat. The same sort of thing happens in people who smoke, drink, gamble, swear, eat too much dessert, yell at their children, and so on.

Simply stated, we train our brains. The brain kick-starts with a stimulus. We respond by buying the Diet Coke. Then we drink it. The brain gets its reward. It's just like Pavlov's dog.

Let me make clear that one of *my* triggers is Diet Coke. (Especially if there is coconut flavoring close by.) Yours might be something entirely different. Yours might be a screaming kid in the checkout line or a hundred-year-old driver weaving aimlessly about or somebody telling you what to do. Think about it for a minute, and you can identify at least a few of your triggers. They're the things that make you behave in ways you otherwise wouldn't.

Well, here's the good news. You can *stop* behaving that way. You can stop leaping tall buildings in a single bound to get some chocolate. You can stop wanting to scream at the lady in the checkout line who is writing a check. (Who still uses checks?!) You can stop nearly experiencing a one-car rollover—yours!—because you're so furious at the punk in the sports car. You can learn to control how you respond to any stimulus.

The key is something called *mindfulness*. It's *being aware* that your brain has just encountered a stimulus. Then, instead of *responding* to the stimulus, mindfulness is realizing, *That was a stimulus*. It's saying to yourself, *I know what to do right now—and I'm* not *going to respond the way I usually do. No automatic behavior today. I'm in control.*

Sounds easy, doesn't it? But you know it's not. Once the brain encounters a stimulus, the reward center in your brain goes crazy. Your heart beats faster and your glands start releasing adrenaline into your blood. Your brain is on hyperalert, expecting its little body to do exactly what it always does. Because, come on now—we need what we need! I need to eat that—I need to vocalize this insulting thought—I need to buy that even though I can't afford it. Of course you don't really need to do any of those things, but, boy, you sure feel like you do.

You will encounter stimuli every day—everything from billboards to stomach pains to angry drivers. Everyone does. But here's the awesome part: you can train your brain to respond how you want it to respond.

When you become mindful, an interesting thing happens: you're suddenly in control again. You're no longer excited about the potential reward. Try this fact on for size: cigarette smokers who become mindful suddenly realize that cigarettes taste like chemicals—not nearly as good as they once thought. Smoking that cigarette may fire up the reward center, the one tied in to the stimulus, but it no longer sends a single watt in the direction of the pleasure center. It's the stimulus—the *anticipation* of smoking a cigarette—that creates all the buzz in the brain. And we all know how we exaggerate in anticipation. The actual cigarette? Not as good as we thought it would be. It tastes bad and deposits tar in the lungs and makes the car stink.

It's the same as the trip to Disneyland we talked about in the last chapter. Sometimes the anticipation doesn't live up to reality.

Once you become mindful and resolve to respond in a different way, an amazing thing happens. You are in control. You no longer have a knee-jerk reaction when a stimulus rears its ugly head. You think—deeply—about what's going on and how you're going to respond. You become more patient. And the more you practice this skill, the more patient you become. The slam dunk? The more patient you are, the happier you will be.

The Microwave

The great teachers say that if you're trying to teach something, use a story to illustrate your point. Why? People remember stories. There's something about a story that just gets you firing on all pistons. Jesus told story after story after story. Stories can teach powerful principles in a memorable way. And that's why I'm going to share a story with you here. Even though this story demonstrates one of my worst moments when it comes to patience, I'm willing to share it because I know you're going to remember it. Forever. Let's just keep it between us though, okay?

Besides humiliating me, this story is going to help you notice stimuli. It will help you figure out how, when confronted by a stimulus, one can either surrender to a bad behavior or make a different choice. A better choice. A choice that will lead to happiness instead of to wherever the stimulus leads.

> When confronted by a stimulus, you can either surrender to a bad behavior or make a different choice. A better choice.

Because in the story I'm about to tell, it sure didn't lead to happiness for me. At least not at first.

Let me set the stage. Sara and I were completely stressed out. There wasn't a cell in our bodies that wasn't stressed. Even our hair was stressed. You see, we were moving. And don't think Sara and I are just a couple of wimps. All the scientists confirm it: moving is one of the top five stressors for us as humans. It's right up there with a major illness, getting a divorce, changing or losing a job, and losing a loved one to death. Yup. Moving. It's that stressful. *Stimulus one.*

You know what it's like to move. At first, you have this grandiose plan that you are going to label every box with exact precision, providing a brilliant description of what's inside. And you are going to put each box exactly where it belongs in the new place, avoiding any chaos as you unpack. You anticipate perfection. Then reality sets in. By the end you're shoving everything under the sun into a bunch of random cardboard boxes because you're in such a hurry to just be done with it. And the folks in your new ward? They just want to get home, back to what they were doing before your moving truck showed up, so with a hearty smile, they dump the boxes anywhere they can. Even the boxes you've labeled. Kitchen boxes end up in the upstairs bathroom, and food storage ends up in the master bedroom closet.

Yeah, that's what happened to us. We couldn't find anything. We had clothes in the kitchen, pots and pans in my daughter's bedroom. That's when I told myself, *Okay, I'm fine. This is fine.* I didn't believe it either. Things really weren't going as planned. *Stimulus two.*

I finally started clearing counter space in the kitchen because I knew the natives would be getting restless and at some point we were going to have to eat. What luck! The next box I opened contained the microwave. I took the microwave out of the box, set it on the counter, and plugged it in. After all, everyone needs a microwave. And anyone with opposable thumbs can make *something* to eat with a microwave.

About that time Sara came into the kitchen. She eyed the microwave, looked at me, and said, "Oh, you can put the microwave back in the box. We're getting a new one."

"Oh, is this one broken?" I asked.

In response, Sara said something that had never occurred to me: "No, it's not broken. It doesn't match."

My mind went into word-association mode. Match. Strike a match. Light something. "You mean we need to *light* the microwave?" I asked Sara. And in my mind I'm thinking, *I've never seen anyone light a microwave. What planet are you from?*

Sara, who was in fact firmly rooted on planet earth, did an Olympic-worthy eye roll. *Stimulus three.* Her stress had now morphed into a tiny bit of frustration. "Hank, describe for me the exterior of the dishwasher."

Stress notwithstanding, I was up for this. "Stainless steel."

"Good. Now describe for me the exterior of the stove."

"Stainless steel. What does this have to do with lighting the microwave?"

"Describe, if you will, the exterior of the refrigerator."

"Stainless steel."

"And what color is the *microwave*?" she asked triumphantly.

"White. Can we get back to lighting the microwave?"

Wait.

All of a sudden it all clicked. It was, as you can guess, the click heard 'round the world. "Oh, you want everything to be the same *color*?"

Thinking her job was done, Sara nodded her head.

"Oh, that doesn't matter," I scoffed. And I plugged the microwave back in.

"It *does* matter," she said as she unplugged it. *Stimulus four.*

Remember, we were both stressed. Stimuli are now everywhere. I told Sara it did *not* matter—only to people who are so hoity-toity that they actually care what other people think. When I get stressed I may at times become passive-aggressive and sarcastic.

Well, the next time I came in the room the microwave was back in the box. I took the microwave out of the box, put it on the counter, and plugged it back in.

The next thing I knew, the microwave was in the box, which was taped securely and sitting in a corner of the garage. I brought the box in the house, ripped all that tape off, took the microwave out of the box, put it on the counter, and plugged it in. That's when my oldest daughter asked, "Are you guys fighting?"

"Nah," I said as casually as I could, being under all that stress. "Mom and Dad aren't fighting; Mom and Dad are in *love*."

These shenanigans went on for another couple of days.

My oldest daughter asked, "Are you guys fighting?" "Nah," I said as casually as I could, being under all that stress. "Mom and Dad aren't fighting; Mom and Dad are in *love*."

We finally decided to compromise.

By deciding to get a new microwave.

(A teenage boy who heard this story once said, "That's not a compromise." I responded, "You're not married.")

Brief aside here about compromise in marriage: I hate cats. I really do. Definitely not my favorite. But Sara loves cats. She really does. So we compromised and we have two cats. I think they should stay where they belong—in the road.

Never mind cats; back to the microwave. Before I go on, though, go back and look at what's happened so far. I helped you identify some of the stimuli to which I was responding—things that caused a knee-jerk reaction in me. Can you think of a way one of us (okay, probably me) could have used mindfulness to choose to react with greater patience?

Have you ever had a time when you were nearly knocked off your feet by a stimulus? That's what was happening to me. I could *feel* it. *I'm not thinking well, and I'm going to say something I don't mean. Something I'll regret later.* I could sense my prefrontal cortex pulsing with impatience.

So that's the condition *I* was in when Sara picked out her dream microwave online, printed out a picture of it, and asked me to go to Home Depot and get it for her.

"Please don't make me pick it up," I pleaded. "I don't even *want* the new microwave. *You* go pick it up."

Sara wasn't bending. "Don't make me go to the store with the kids." I had to admit she had a point—going to the store with a bunch of little kids complicates life by about five billion times. My kids have often asked for ten different things by the time we're halfway down the first aisle. I have one child that stopped asking altogether and just puts what he wants in the cart, hoping it will somehow make it home with us.

So we compromised.

Again.

I went to Home Depot, clutching the little picture of the microwave, and headed straight to the display of microwaves under fifty dollars. After an exhaustive search, I failed to find Sara's chosen microwave.

I moved on to the microwaves under a hundred dollars. Again, my search was fruitless. I got sucked deeper and deeper into the dazzling displays of microwaves until I finally reached the only-people-who-are-already-hoity-toity-and-care-what-people-think display. Like I said, I get a little passive-aggressive. Sure enough, there was Sara's microwave. *Stimulus five!*

Great.

At that point, I should have been mindful that lots of semihostile chemicals were flooding my body and I was getting upset. But, oh no. I did nothing to circumvent it, and I started responding. Now I was mad. I grabbed the box and stomped to the

Now I was mad. I grabbed the box and stomped to the front of the store. I put it down on the checkout counter. Maybe a little too firmly.

front of the store. I put it down on the checkout counter. Maybe a little too firmly.

The checkout clerk smiled at me. "Welcome to Home Depot."

"Yep," I snarled with a fake smile.

Did I mention I tend to get a little sarcastic when I get upset? I may have been hungry, too, so cut me some slack.

"Oh, wow." There she was, face-to-face with the ideal customer. The one every checkout person dreams about helping.

You can just imagine what happened next. I stormed out to the parking lot, shoved that stupid box into the car, and drove home. I thundered into the house, almost tripped going up the stairs from the garage, and set it on the counter, right in front of Sara. At that point, all I could manage was a single word and a very counterfeit smile: "Microwave."

"Thanks, Sweetie," she cooed. Sure. I'm no dummy. *Sweetie* here means "idiot." I was being mocked. *Stimulus six.*

About ten minutes later I was in my room doing something that really mattered when I heard Sara tearing into the microwave box. And then her voice pierced over the airwaves and shattered the tiny bit of calm I had managed to come to: "*What did you buy*?"

"A microwave."

"Yeah, but it's a *blue* microwave!"

My eyes snapped shut. Deep breath.

No. No it's not. "It's stainless steel," I called to her, eyes still shut. "It says so on the box."

"I *know* what it says on the box," she said more loudly than I would have guessed she could, "but it's BLUE. Come in here. Look for yourself."

You can just imagine my fury as I went to the kitchen, can't you? *Stimulus seven.*

Sure enough. The microwave was blue. *Stimulus eight.*

And you know what's coming next. Every husband on the planet knows what's coming next.

"Take it back."

"Okay. I'll take it back tomorrow."

"We need a microwave tonight."

"Just use the old one. Just for tonight."

"I can't. I sold it."

"*What?*"

"I sold it for five dollars."

Stimulus nine.

Around this point, my sarcasm turned into silence. Being the good husband I am, I picked up the blue microwave and started carrying it out to the car. And right then my wife—the woman I absolutely love and adore and worship with all my heart and soul—had the audacity to say, "Take the kids."

Stimulus ten. Blast off.

Trigger pulled. Now I'm mad, and I don't care who knows it.

Suddenly I had a bunch of little kids hanging on my legs as I tried to balance the microwave and them down the stairs and out to the car. It's a miracle no one was seriously injured, including me.

I wasn't myself anymore—I walked into the store stone-faced, my kids running to keep up, and I absolutely threw that microwave onto the counter. It almost went off the other side of the counter into the arms of the customer service woman. I thought I heard something break. And I was *glad,* because I *wanted* to break it. No smiling, no friendliness, no Christlike behavior here—just mad Hank. He doesn't come out very often (once with a highway patrolman in Idaho, once at a third-grade basketball game, and once with a police officer in Virginia) (oh, and once at a ticket counter of an airline), but when he does, it's not pretty. He's actually downright irrational. I hope you can identify somewhat with this. (Oh, and once with a teenager when I was a brand-new seminary teacher . . . he deserved it, though.)

You're probably feeling pretty embarrassed for me right now. I don't blame you. I'm sure people were getting their phones out to video the freak show at the customer service desk.

The customer service woman asked calmly, "Can I help you?" She had one eye glued to the box I had slammed down on the counter, the other glued nervously to me. No one wants to be tomorrow's headline.

"THE MICROWAVE'S BLUE!" I exploded. My kids grew very quiet.

"'Scuse me?"

By this time all I could manage was staccato phrases in angry tones. "Microwave's blue. Says stainless steel. Package was wrong.

> You're probably pretty embarrassed for me right now. I don't blame you. I'm sure people were getting out their cell phones to video the freak show at the customer service desk.

Need another microwave."

Well, this customer service representative—let's call her Amy—was a pro. She was used to dealing with people who can't control their emotions. And she didn't respond in a negative way. No, Amy stayed calm and happy. (We irrational and impatient people really hate you mindful people sometimes.) And that's when she smiled and said, "Oh, no. I'm so sorry. Okay. Can I have your receipt, please?"

I should tell you that my little stress-induced display was intense enough to attract attention. Not just from my kids, and not just from other customers. Before I knew it, Amy's supervisor, we'll call him Derek, was right by us, asking coolly, "What seems to be the problem?"

I sighed and stared. Thinlipped. I gave a slight nod of acknowledgment.

Good old Amy patiently explained to Derek what was going on.

"Okay, we're so sorry about that, sir," Derek said. "We're going to get that taken care of for you."

Another slight nod of acknowledgment. *Yeah, sure you are. I'll bet.* Lips were definitely pressed thin. I could feel it. My day, my wallet, and my marriage had been terribly interrupted by this mess, and my impatience was showing on my face.

I will remember what happened next for the rest of my life. Derek took a few steps away, had an idea, came to an abrupt halt, turned back to me, and asked, "Hey, did you remove the blue cellophane from the microwave?"

Insert record screech here.

Amy looked up from the register and looked at him. Then she looked at me.

There was a long, quiet pause as I took in what he said.

They were both looking at me, not moving.

More pause.

More silence.

I swallowed, breathed deeply, tilted my head slightly, and said, "The what?"

I was speaking much more calmly than I was just thirty seconds earlier.

"Stainless steel appliances come wrapped in blue cellophane to protect the finish. Here. Let me take a look."

He opened the box and started peeling the blue cellophane off the stainless steel microwave. "The microwave's not blue," he said, stating what was by now pathetically obvious. "It's just the cellophane."

He smiled.

Have you ever seen someone who is in a very desperate situation trying not to laugh? Oh, it wasn't Derek the supervisor. And it for *sure* wasn't me. It was Amy, the customer service clerk I had almost knocked over with a microwave a few minutes ago. She looked like she was chewing something that was trying to escape from her mouth. Her face was crimson. Her eyes were starting to water. But she'd soared through the Home Depot training, and she knew you never laugh at a customer.

Have you ever seen someone in a very desperate situation trying not to laugh? The customer service clerk looked like she was chewing something that was trying to escape from her mouth.

Just then from about my thigh level came a small but loud, young voice: "Wait, Dad, the microwave's not blue?"

"Quiet, please," I said through gritted teeth.

"Dad, you said these people were idiots."

"I know. Stop talking. Go find something. I'll buy it for you. Go!"

I had only one thing left to do. I picked up the microwave—you know, the one with a broken glass plate inside—and I walked away from the desk. As I was about fifty feet away, I heard Amy erupt in laughter and sputter to some other employees, "Come over here! You've gotta hear this!"

Amy and her associates weren't the only ones who got a good laugh out of the whole thing. Guess who else thought it was hilarious? Guess who else thought it was the funniest thing she'd ever heard?

Yup. My wife. When I got home and told her the story, she was laughing so hard she could barely speak. Apparently her hearing was affected as well, because she kept making me start over.

In my defense, I said, "Sara, you thought it was blue too!"

"I know," she wheezed, "but I didn't *take it back*!"

It was an episode with staying power. Weeks later, we'd be driving somewhere when all of a sudden Sara would start to giggle. "You thought it was blue!" Sara laughs. Kids laugh. Hank doesn't laugh.

Okay, I admit it. This story has provided the fodder for lots of entertainment for friends and audiences. (Our family friends Jake and Heather are the ones who convinced me I had to tell the story publicly.) But it has also made me stop and think of a *lot* of times about where I should have drawn the line. Where I should have stopped in my tracks and said to myself, *Wait, my brain is going crazy right now, and whatever comes out of my mouth is not going to reflect the real me*. I should have recognized that I was not about to be normal. I should have kept my mouth shut.

There were also lots of points—I counted at least ten stimuli—at which I should have stopped, taken a deep breath, and said to myself, *This is not that big a deal. This is fine. I'm okay.* But, no. Somehow I had managed to take a somewhat bothersome situation and turn it into a personal humiliation. For no good reason. None at all.

Maybe you've been in this kind of situation yourself. Maybe you, like I, had some pretty embarrassing time to reflect later. You know. *I shouldn't have said that. I shouldn't have acted that way. That never should have happened. I was out of control. I wasn't thinking. Wow, I feel so dumb right now.*

A few weeks after the microwave incident, I was listening to general conference. Have you ever had a general conference speaker give a talk that had you convinced they had been watching your life? I have. It happened at the very next conference. In fact, I was certain President Dieter F. Uchtdorf had been working a temp job with Amy at the customer service desk at Home Depot the night I stormed in with the "blue" microwave.

During that April 2010 general conference address, President Uchtdorf called impatience "a symptom of selfishness." As if that wasn't bad enough, he said it was also "a trait of the self-absorbed. It arises from the all-too-prevalent condition called 'center of the universe' syndrome, which leads people to believe that the world revolves around them and that all others are just supporting cast in the grand theater of mortality in which only they have the starring role."

My mind raced back to the microwave episode. As I went over the whole sordid thing in my mind, I realized he was describing me. I had "center of the universe" syndrome. All that plugging in the microwave over and over and stomping around with boxes and snarling at Home Depot employees. That was me. Instead of having even a miniscule shred of patience, I had decided *I was the center of the universe.* It was all about me; my wants, my needs, my time. When I made it all about me, happiness was completely out of reach.

I hope you can see now why patience is so tied to happiness. I should have been better. I should have been more patient. I *know* I would have been happier. President Hinckley once taught, "Generally speaking, the most miserable people I know are those who are obsessed with themselves; the happiest people I know are those who lose themselves in the service of others."

The lesson will always stay with me and I hope it stays with you. It is nearly impossible to be selfish and be happy.

Patience with Divinity

Let's switch gears here and talk about a different aspect of patience. My microwave story is a great example of the most simple kind of patience—the kind that keeps you from flipping out when you think you have a blue microwave and all you really wanted was the old white one. The one somebody got for five bucks. There is a much more important kind of patience: the kind that causes you to allow the Lord to do His work in His due time. Because *that* kind of patience is also directly hardwired into happiness.

Why? Because the Lord knows what He's doing, and we *don't* know His mind or His purposes. But remember? He told us *our* purpose is to have joy—to be happy. And even if we think He's forgotten about us or if He's just not working stuff out quickly enough, we need to know with all our hearts that He's got this. We need to be patient with Him. In fact, one of my favorite sayings is, "When you find yourself losing patience with God, remember how patient He has been with you."

> Even if we think the Lord has forgotten about us or is not working stuff out quickly enough, we need to know with all our hearts that He's got this.

Let me give you an example with which I think you can relate. Maybe all your children are perfect and all the people you love are still clinging to the iron rod right next to you. If so, I'm sure you can think of *someone* who's struggling with a wayward kid or a rebellious sister or a defiant spouse. That's one of the most painful experiences in this world. One that teaches you patience as much as any experience I know of.

Now remember that the Lord referred to His Church as "the vineyard" in the parable of the vineyard (see Matthew 20:1–16). In this parable, as in real life, you've got lots of people working their hearts out in the vineyard—in the Church—but you also have a bunch of people outside the vineyard. You know what I mean—these are the ones who have left the vineyard or have never had the opportunity to even start working there. Some of them have been out there in the marketplace for a very long time. They are stressed. Maybe one or two of them are precious to you; though you've been working away in the vineyard this whole time, you've never stopped watching. Checking. Praying. Hoping.

Some consider this a parable for a grieving mother. If you're that grieving mother (or father, for that matter), you know that all you can do is keep the faith. Be patient. Eternity is a long time and the Lord knows what He is doing. Keep praying. Keep believing. Because you don't know if or when the Lord is going to walk through that marketplace and embrace *your* worker—bring *your* worker home.

I will testify that He will. In His own due time. It might, as the parable taught, be at the eleventh hour. At the end of the day, all the workers receive the same reward, whether they started in the first hour or the eleventh. The Lord is aware of every single person out there in the marketplace. He's also aware of every single person in the vineyard. And He has His purposes for every single one. The Lord is going to give them multiple opportunities to come to work. Our job is to have patience, to work hard in our assigned spot, and trust His timing.

The Lord is aware of every single person out there in the marketplace. He's also aware of every single person in the vineyard. And He has His purposes for every single one.

In his October 2000 general conference talk, Elder Dallin H.

Oaks provided a really cool perspective on the whole vineyard-marketplace parable. He said that "the Master's reward in the Final Judgment will not be based on how long we have labored in the vineyard. We do not obtain our heavenly reward by punching a time clock. What is essential is that our labors in the workplace of the Lord have caused us to *become* something. For some of us, this requires a longer time than for others. What is important in the end is what we have become by our labors."

So here it is, something lots of us may not have considered: "Many who come in the eleventh hour have been refined and prepared by the Lord in ways *other* than formal employment in the vineyard." Then he said that these workers are like pancake mix "to which it is only necessary to 'add water'—the perfecting ordinance of baptism and the gift of the Holy Ghost. With that addition—even in the eleventh hour—these workers are in the same state of development and qualified to receive the same reward as those who have labored long in the vineyard."

Imagine that: Maybe you've been a member of the Church all your life and worked away in your little section of the vineyard because the Lord looked at you and said, "This one is going to need a lot of time in the oven to become a saint!" Maybe that child of yours or sibling of yours or spouse of yours is having the right experiences outside the vineyard that will one day make them like pancake mix: just add water, and *voila*! Qualified for the kingdom. You don't know. I don't know. Only the Lord knows, and it's up to us to have patience with that divine process.

It is never too late for the Lord to bring back those that we love.

When the Savior arrived in Bethany four days after his friend Lazarus had died, many said it was "too late." "If he'd arrived just a day earlier," the Jews thought, "Lazarus's spirit would still be close and could return to his body." But in their minds too much time had gone by. But it wasn't too late for the Lord. He did the impossible. He brought back someone they thought was unreachable, unhealable, and too far away. It is never too late for the Lord to bring back those we love.

I'd liked to wrap up this chapter on patience with some thoughts President Henry B. Eyring shared in his October 2013 general conference address, which he tenderly titled, "To My Grandchildren." Years earlier, a friend of his had spoken about his grandmother—a solid worker in the vineyard, a woman of faith who had lived a life of devotion, never even coming close to straying out of the vineyard.

Sadly, however, this good woman's much-loved grandson had not made the same kinds of choices. In fact, his choices couldn't have been much more radically different than those of his grandmother. He lived a life of crime. And he was eventually sentenced to prison.

I want to you capture in your mind's eye this sweet, clean, righteous grandmother driving her old sedan along the lonesome highway on her way to visit her grandson in prison. Do you think there were worry lines skipping around her mouth? Can you just see the tears sliding down her cheeks as she prayed out loud with anguish, "I've tried to live a good life. Why, why do I have this tragedy of a grandson who seems to have destroyed his life?"

Into her mind came an answer that all of us need to remember as we strive to exercise patience with the Lord: "I gave him to you because I knew you could and would love him no matter what he did."

Life was never meant to be easy. But our abilities will be sufficient to see us through the difficulties as long as we stay mindful of *His* abilities and we exercise patience in the process.

I'm sure you realize that life was never meant to be easy. Life is a lot of things, but unchallenging definitely isn't one of them. Mortal life often asks a lot of us. A lot more than we think we can give. Our abilities will be sufficient to see us through the difficulties as long as we stay mindful of His abilities and as long as we exercise patience in the process. The Atonement of Christ not only cleanses us from sin but enables us to push forward with patience. If we firmly attach ourselves to Him, we will know greater happiness than we can ever imagine.

CHAPTER FIVE

Don't Forget Contention—And We're Still Not Done with Patience

OH, GREAT. JUST WHEN YOU thought it was safe to go back in the water, here it comes again. *Patience.* Only this time it's all tied up in a neat little package with something else that tremendously impacts happiness: contention.

What exactly is *contention*? Contention is the firstborn son of impatience. It can range all the way from disagreement and dissension to an altercation, conflict, or out-and-out war. We'll check out how it ties in to patience a little later. For now, let's see how it impacts happiness.

When the air is sizzling with contention, people feel unsafe, unloved, and disrespected. And when people feel unsafe, unloved, and disrespected, they do nasty things (like throw microwaves.) They start doing things they'd never do with their normal brain, right? Sadly, we often fail to recognize that when someone flips out (or looks like he's going to any minute), he or she is simply feeling unsafe.

Unfortunately, when someone feels unsafe, unloved, and disrespected, they often treat others in a mean, unloving, and disrespectful way. They often demean you. Or try to talk over you and interrupt you with a bunch of rapid-fire arguments. Instead of being mindful—stopping and trying to figure out how to make things safe—we take their behavior personally. We get angry and then we ratchet the contention up a notch by matching their behavior. Because, hey, that's a lot easier to do. And things just go from bad to worse. Nobody in their right mind enjoys it when this cycle of contention takes over. I don't, you don't, and happiness doesn't.

Once again, the scriptures are pretty clear on contention (as they are on so many things). The Savior warned the Nephites about the dangers of contention when He said, "He that hath the spirit of contention is not of me, but is of the devil, who is the father of contention" (3 Nephi 11:29). Remember the technique of embedded messages? There's a big one right there. God doesn't cause, or like, or see any advantage in contention. Satan does. So if contention is going on, you would be smart to put on the mindful brakes for a minute and figure out exactly what's happening.

Here's another message embedded in that short verse: if you want to be happy, avoid contention like the plague. Because that's what it is—it's a plague. In fact, contention and happiness are polar opposites—one leads away from the other.

Remember the people in 4 Nephi? The prophet-historian Mormon described the people by writing, "There could not be a happier people among all the people who had been created by the hand of God" (4 Nephi 1:16)?

We've already talked about some of the reasons these people were so astonishingly happy. I'd like to now focus in on one particular reason for that happiness: they had "no contention" among them. Having no contention was such an important factor, in fact, that it is mentioned *four times* in that very brief book (see verses 2, 13, 15, and 18). And in one of the verses, Mormon tells us *why* there was no contention: "because of the love of God which did dwell in the hearts of the people" (4 Nephi 1:15). There's an embedded message in that verse that speaks loud and clear about how to be happy: we need to do all we can to deepen our love for our Heavenly Father. Often we try to develop love for each other without first trying to develop love of God. Often we try to make our children love each other when we really need to help them learn

If you want to be happy, avoid contention like the plague. Because that's what it is—it's a plague.

to love God. Because often, it's the love of God that leads us to love each other.

How does that happen? It's a simple yet complicated form of divine arithmetic: "And we have known and believed the love that God hath to us. . . . We love him, because he first loved us" (1 John 4:16, 19). There you have it, simple as that: we love Him because He first loved us. We're being reminded here that it's not too tough to love someone who genuinely loves us. And no one loves us like God loves us. Once we integrate that truth into our character, our behavior begins to match our beliefs.

But it doesn't stop there. Let's go on to step two, if you will: if the love of God dwells in our heart, we automatically try our very best to love the people around us as God loves them. A mighty change of heart leads to a mighty change of behavior.

Yes, we're mortals. Sure, we have limits. No, none of us has ever perfected the love God has for His sons and daughters. That's why He's God and we're not. We may not even be able to adequately wrap our heads around that kind of love. But I feel pretty confident in saying that every one of us could do *better* when it comes to being more loving, especially in our own homes.

I remember with great hilarity a spoof done at one of our ward parties. The bishop's wife and a couple of her friends stood on stage and bravely warbled, "There is beauty all around, where there's no one home." I wasn't the only one who saw the truth in their humor. And I'm pretty sure I wasn't the only one who also felt a little sheepish.

I don't know what your house is like, but I know what *my* house is like, and I know that we have our ups and downs when it comes to loving each other with a pure, sweet, constant kind of love. I take that back: we all love each other, but sometimes we have a difficult time *showing* it. I think my kids have a pretty easy time loving God. After all, *He's God*. He's accepting and loving and doesn't break their stuff or eat all the dessert or stand in front of the TV when a movie is on. But loving a little brother who does all those things every day?

Okay, that's pretty normal when you're dealing with a six-year-old and a four-year-old. Neither of their brains is fully developed, and they just don't have those feelings all the time. Has that ever happened in your house? I've watched that happen, and I've watched parents try to *force* their children to show how much they love each other. The tactics are kind of hilarious when you really think about it. You make a couple of little kids sit on the stairs holding hands for forty-five minutes or until they love each other, whichever comes last. Or you shut them in the closet or the laundry room together until they show how much they love each other (or, more likely, until they *tell* you they love each other, shouted out through the door, as if that's any guarantee). Or here's one of my favorites: the dreaded contention shirt.

Here's how it works: when you catch two of your kids embroiled in contention—you know, a disagreement or dissension or an altercation or even out-and-out combat—you put those two kids into a big shirt together until they figure out how to get along and confess their undying love for each other. Really? Isn't that like wrapping two scrabbling cats in a bath towel? What if your boss made you do that with the coworker who drives you crazy? What if the bishop had you do that with the ward member you don't like? Would it work?

I mean, honestly. If someone put me in a shirt with somebody else I wasn't getting along with, I don't think it would make me like him. In fact, it would be so awkward I doubt I could even achieve eye contact. I may have a conversation about hairy arms, but that'd probably be as far as I'd get to a real friendship.

So how *can* you decrease contention and increase love in your home? Instead of trying to force your children to love each other, help them love God. What's the first step? Focus on helping your kids see all the ways in which God loves *them*. Talk about it during family home evening, car rides, and camping trips. Mention

So how *can* you decrease contention and increase love in your home? Instead of trying to force your children to love each other, help them love God.

the love of God in your personal and family prayers. Make sure it is talked about in priesthood blessings. Give the Holy Ghost as many opportune moments as possible to testify to your children that they are loved more than they can possibly imagine.

You know what comes next. They'll love Him back. And because of their love for God, their feelings begin to naturally change—and that includes their feelings for other people. Even their brothers and sisters. They see people differently—even their brothers and sisters. And if things progress like the scriptures indicate they will, there will be love, even without contention shirts. And where there is safety, love, and respect, there is happiness.

The Patience Journal

Okay, I threatened to drag you back to patience, and here goes. Why? A lot of contention is caused by impatience. If you're living in the same world I am, you have plenty of chances—probably every day—to see (and maybe even experience) impatience and how it causes contention. Am I the only one who has been in a hurry but been stuck in the customer line behind a woman with an entire folding wallet stuffed with coupons? How is it I always end up in those lines? My impatience in that situation leads to all kinds of contention. Here's proof: I'm usually less than chirpy with the clerk by the time I finally get there, to put it mildly. And, okay, I'll admit I want to rip that wallet of coupons out of that woman's hands and set it on fire. *There should be a designated lane for people with more than fifty coupons. They'd probably love it. They like each other. They could talk about all the money they save!*

And what about all those telephone solicitation calls? You're right in the middle of mixing your meatloaf, and your hands are covered with all kinds of unmentionable goo—because the only way to properly mix a meatloaf is with your bare hands, of course—and the phone starts ringing. You manage to pick up a corner of the phone without spreading the threat of horrific disease only to find out that someone on the other end wants to sell you a solar panel system or wants to know who you are voting for in the school board election. Suddenly you want to smash something—hard—and you may or may not be very nice to your eleven-year-old who is right then begging for a Popsicle. (Try doing what I do with phone solicitors: hand the phone to your three-year-old and say, "It's Grandpa.")

Or how about this. You've got exactly nine minutes to get to the drive-up window at the bank before it closes, and you're stuck behind a grandma who doesn't look like she can see over the steering wheel, going ten miles per hour below the speed limit. Not only that, but she doesn't register that the light turned green a full minute ago (probably because she was looking through her coupons), and who are you to blast your horn so loudly that she then becomes paralyzed with fear (or deadened by confusion) and forgets where the gas pedal is?

> When you feel impatient, your brain rapidly morphs to anger and aggression. Your brain then diverts blood to high-priority tasks, like hitting and running.

Yup, impatience creates contention.

Tempers flare. Harsh words are spoken. In the very worst of scenarios, punches are thrown. And nobody—not the intrepid clerk who just spent fifteen minutes sorting coupons, not the eleven-year-old who may never ask for a Popsicle again, not the ancient-of-days woman on the road—is happy. Especially not you.

Let's review some of the biology behind impatience because it will help you see exactly how it creates contention and how you can stop it. When you feel impatient, your brain rapidly morphs to anger and aggression. At that point, your brain diverts blood from activities it deems nonessential (like rational thinking) to high-priority tasks, like hitting and running. That's right: most of your blood flows away from your skull and into your arms and legs, so you can do what your primitive ancestors did: fight or flee. It worked great for them—it kept them alive—but it's not so useful for you. Because when you're stuck in line behind the coupon-wielding shopper, it's a sure bet you're not going to be punching your way to the head of the line, taking out coupon woman in the process.

Here's when mindfulness comes in again: You need to learn to recognize that you're feeling impatient, getting angry, wanting to do something irrational. You need to learn to *stop*. Regain control. Take the steps you need to take to turn your brain back on, get the blood flowing back upstairs. You need to learn to constantly monitor yourself. Ask, *What's happening to me right now? How can I turn this around?* God gave us frontal lobes, and He expects us to use them.

It's what the gospel has been teaching us all along. Long ago, the writer of Proverbs declared, "A soft answer turneth away wrath: but grievous words stir up anger" (Proverbs 15:1). I'm guessing he was referring to the kind of "grievous words" that get exchanged when impatience leads to contention. In our dispensation, President Gordon B. Hinckley, in a satellite broadcast for husbands and wives ,encouraged us, "Cultivate the art of the soft answer. It will bless your homes, it will bless your lives, it will bless your companionships, it will bless your children."

In that same satellite broadcast, President Hinckley clarified, "There is need for much discipline in marriage, not of one's companion but of one's self. Husbands, wives, remember, 'He [or she] that is slow to anger is better than the mighty' (Proverbs 16:32)." I don't know about you, but I'm always a lot more willing to try to change my poor wife than I am to change myself—but that's not where happiness is.

A few decades earlier, President David O. McKay—author of *Secrets of a Happy Life*—admonished, "Let husband and wife never speak to one another in loud tones, unless the house is on fire." I don't often get loud, but I do get sarcastic—which can be even more damaging. I'm embarrassed to admit that I remember traces of sarcasm in the Great Microwave Debacle (by *traces* I mean *loads*), yet I don't remember the house ever being on fire—I'm glad I didn't try to light the microwave.

You know, before I became a parent, I thought I was the epitome of patience. I was one of those people who saw someone upset with a child and thought, "When I'm a parent, I'll *never* get that way with my kids." Now I realize that parenthood has given me a front-row seat to my own immaturity—a grand balcony outlook on my own foolishness. And having twins has notched that up by a mile. My wife is the personification of patience with our children, but I have a long way to go. The good news is that, like everyone else on this planet, I'm a work in progress and the Lord is okay with that. The important part is to keep working on it.

Now that you understand what contention does to happiness and how impatience leads to contention, I'm hoping you'll accept a little challenge if you struggle in this area. It has to do with patience, but it has a little twist. You'll see what I mean in a minute.

I'd like you to keep a Patience Journal for two weeks. For the next two weeks, your job is to focus on how much patience you have. Here's the twist: your job is not to become more patient—your job is to become more *mindful* about how much patience you have.

Here's how it works. Every day for two weeks, write a few sentences about a situation you were in that required patience. Include how you felt and how you acted. It's most effective if you can write your thoughts soon after they occur; if you wait until it's time for bed, you've probably calmed down quite a bit, and your recollection may not be as accurate as it will be while adrenaline is still surging through your veins.

Let's say you were on your way to the store because you ran out of sesame seeds for a Thai dish you were making for dinner. You were in a bit of a hurry. Instead of being *able* to hurry, you got stuck behind a man who for all intents and purposes might have been on a Sunday drive to enjoy the scenery. He held you up at two intersections. Then, as you approached the store, he suddenly stopped, nearly causing a rear-end collision—and the rear end wasn't yours.

This might be your entry in your Patience Journal for the day: *I was in a hurry to get to the store but got stuck behind a slow-as-tar man who was crawling along at twenty mph. Then right as we got to the place you turn in to the store parking lot, he slammed on the brakes. With no rhyme or reason. I was miraculously able to stop instead of plowing into him. I laid on the horn, screamed at him, and even waved my arm out the window.*

Way to write an honest report! Your impatience caused you to label him. It also caused you to honk for all you were worth, even say a few choice things. It was a classic case of impatience. Contention. Unhappiness. But now that you've written it down, it's also a classic example of mindfulness.

Do it for two weeks. I'm pretty sure you'll be surprised at what starts happening. When stuff like this occurs, you'll actually be mindful of what's happening *while it's happening*. The next time it happens, you just might take a minute to slow down and change your reaction. You might be more mindful that it's happening, and you might just do things differently. And you will almost certainly feel happier. There is a quiet confidence that comes from self-control.

I say that because a group of people was paid to do exactly what I'm asking you to do. Don't worry, you'll still get the benefit, even if I'm not shelling out any cash. This group of people kept their Patience Journal for two weeks. They recorded times when their patience was tested and how they responded. The researchers tested them before and after their journaling experience. And guess what? After keeping that journal for just two weeks, these people had actually changed their own behavior. A series of tests proved that they were now more patient.

And, as you know by now, patience leads to happiness.

There's a lot more to patience—more than I can possibly include in a couple of chapters. But this will have to do for now. In his April 2010 general conference address, President Dieter F. Uchtdorf said:

> Patience is a godly attribute that can heal souls, unlock treasures of knowledge and understanding, and transform ordinary men and women into saints and angels. . . . Patience means . . . reining in anger and holding back the unkind word. . . . Patience means accepting that which cannot be changed and facing it with courage, grace, and faith. . . .
>
> Patience is a process of perfection. The Savior Himself said that in your patience you possess your souls. Or, to use another translation of the Greek text, in your patience you *win mastery* of your souls.

To me, that not only describes patience, it is also a beautiful description of happiness.

CHAPTER SIX

Depression: Why You Can't Just "Snap Out of It"

You can't discuss happiness without talking about depression. Because for people who have depression, happiness may seem desperately and painfully out of reach. Happiness becomes a sensitive subject—talking about it often bringing tears of frustration.

You may be thinking right now: *I'm not depressed. I don't need this chapter.*

I'm begging you not to do that. Even if *you're* not depressed, chances are good you know someone who is (you'll find out why in just a minute). And I know that this chapter will help you understand what is often a very misunderstood problem; it will enable you to offer the empathy and aid that could make a huge difference—perhaps a lifesaving difference—in someone's life.

So thank you for reading this chapter. You'll be glad you did.

Let's start with how we often treat people who are depressed. If you've ever struggled with depression, you've undoubtedly heard all the "helpful" bits of advice that get thrown at depressed people. They even try it on themselves sometimes. Maybe you're guilty of having said some of them yourself:

When life hands you lemons, make lemonade.
Just be happy—it's not that hard.
You're freaking out over nothing.
Remember, there's always someone worse off than you are.
Life's not fair, get used to it.
Count your blessings.
Stop feeling sorry for yourself.
Pull yourself up by your bootstraps.

A person with depression *can't choose* to make their depression go away any more than a person with cancer or diabetes can just choose to make their disease go away.

One thing I've learned is that happiness is a choice.

You can do anything you want if you just set your mind to it.

I totally get it. After [insert sad event], I was so depressed.

Try thinking more positively.

You're being selfish.

I miss the old you.

Or my personal favorite: *Snap out of it!*

All of these myths can now be relegated to the past. We can now call it "The fifteen things not to say to someone with depression." If you are depressed, you *can't* just snap out of it. It doesn't work that way.

You might be thinking, "Hank, a depressed person *chooses* to not snap out of it."

No, they don't. They really *can't*. They *can't choose* to make their depression go away any more than a person with cancer or diabetes can just choose to make their disease go away.

We should probably stop here for a minute to define depression. Everyone has natural ups and downs; it's part of living. Everyone occasionally feels some sadness. Grief naturally occurs when a loved one passes away. Grief is a sign of deep love.

There are countless things that can cause different degrees of sadness. When your pet gets hit by a car (that cat joke from a few chapters ago was probably in poor taste; sorry). When you have a really bad fight with your best friend. When you get laid off from work. Basically, sadness or grief can happen as a result of anything that upsets the normal balance in your life. When those kinds of things happen, you can and *do* snap out of it—eventually. And in those cases, making lemonade, counting your blessings, or choosing to think more positively might just be a cure for you. If that is the case for you, good for you. Be proud of your mental and emotional fortitude.

But here's the important thing to realize: while those feelings can be sad, or might be depressing for a little while, they do *not* constitute *depression.*

Consider for just a minute what you've always thought about depression. Andrew Solomon, who I'll introduce to you more thoroughly a bit later, said, "It's a strange poverty of the English language . . . that we use this same word, *depression,* to describe how a kid feels when it rains on his birthday, and to describe how somebody feels the minute before they commit suicide." In this chapter, we're *not* talking about how a kid feels when it rains on his birthday.

People seem to confuse three things: sadness, grief, and depression. Though they all might seem similar, it is important for us to understand the differences.

Sadness occurs when you are impacted by something that brings on temporary sorrow. You hear that a friend has been diagnosed with cancer. A sense of sadness washes over you as you consider all the difficulty she and her family will have to endure as a result of treatment and recovery. You vow to find a way to serve her. Within a day or two, the busyness of your own life takes over, and you continue on with your responsibilities; your friend's diagnosis is no longer front and center in your consciousness. You feel sad for them when it is brought to your attention and you resolve to help in any way you can.

Grief is the sorrow, suffering, pain, or distress you feel following a loss. It can occur following any kind of loss but is most common following the death of a loved one. Lots of researchers have put a lot of time and effort into trying to figure out grief—and there's no consensus as to how long grief is supposed to last. At first, you may be incredibly unhappy; it may actually be hard for you to function and do the things you're expected to do on a daily basis. That's normal. But as time goes on, your feelings of sadness and pain begin to resolve, and you start feeling better. Not happy, but better. Some say this happens within a month or two; others say it takes a year (or even longer, depending on how close you were to the person who died). That can be normal too. Eventually, though, grief does resolve. You might always feel some sadness as a result of the loss, but it isn't debilitating. You eventually are able to smile again, laugh again, and move forward in your "new normal." Please don't think I'm diminishing how hard grieving can be. The loss of beloved friends and family members is one of the most difficult parts of mortality. It is often physically, mentally, emotionally, and spiritually draining.

We need to be very clear here: sadness and grief are not depression.

Okay, so depression is not sadness or grief. "Hank," you may be thinking, "maybe depressed people are just in a bad mood all the time." I do remember one woman who told me, "I used to think I was in a bad mood, but it's been a few years, so I guess that's just who I am now." We've *all* had to deal with someone who's in a bad mood—and unless you have to chain yourself to the bedpost to prevent being translated every night, you've undoubtedly been in a really bad mood yourself a time or two. I was in a *really* bad mood over that microwave.

Depression is not sadness or grief. Depression is not a bad mood. *Depression* is a biological, chemical problem.

Depression is *not* a bad mood. Mood is adaptive; it changes. It's incredibly valuable for us to experience all the different moods that we do: joy and sadness and fear and delight and anger and humor and optimism, to name just a few. They give dimension to life. A bad mood is not depression. In fact, depression is what happens when that whole "mood system" gets broken. You no longer feel *any* moods.

In fact, some people think that depression means you're simply seeing the world through the haze of a bad mood. They think it's like this gray veil has settled over you, making it impossible to see anything that isn't filtered through that gray veil. *Well, that's easy*, you might be thinking, *just take off the gray veil*! But here's what happens with depression: You can't take off the gray veil because your brain cannot comprehend that it is a veil. Because of the workings of the brain, a depressed person starts to believe that the veil that has been removed, in fact, is the veil of happiness. All that gray? A person with depression thinks that what comes through that gray filter is life as it really is. They see the gray as the truth.

In reality, nothing could be farther from the truth, but their mind is not in state to see it. Even if you try to put it right in front of them.

So if it's not sadness or grief or a really cruddy mood, what *is* depression?

In a landmark address delivered at the October 2013 general conference, Elder Jeffrey R. Holland said:

> When I speak of [depression], I am not speaking of bad hair days, tax deadlines, or other discouraging moments we all have. Everyone is going to be anxious or downhearted on occasion. The Book of Mormon says Ammon and his brethren were depressed at a very difficult time, and so can the rest of us be. But today I am speaking of something more serious, of an affliction so severe that it significantly restricts a person's ability to function fully, a crater in the mind so deep that no one can responsibly suggest it would surely go away if those victims would just square their shoulders and think more positively.

Depression is a biological, chemical problem. It's not something that someone imagines, or makes up, or just decides to be. It's not something you just "get over." In fact, it often gets worse with time. You can see depression very clearly with neuroimaging. It is *not* a character problem; it's a chemistry problem. It is a medical problem. A health problem. That is so crucial to understand that I'll say it again. Depression is not a character problem, it is a chemistry problem. People don't choose to be depressed any more than you would choose to get cancer or choose to have kidney failure. Let me repeat that one more time, because it's critically important: depression

> **You can see depression very clearly with neuroimaging. It is *not* a character problem; it's a chemistry problem. A medical problem. A health problem. That is so critical to understand.**

is not a character problem. It's a chemical problem. A disease.

That's right: depression is a disease. Let me repeat, it's every bit as much of a disease as arthritis or reflux or asthma or celiac disease. And I don't think you'd *ever* tell someone with any of those diseases to just "snap out of it." Of course you wouldn't, because you are a good person. And because you are such a good person, from now on you aren't ever going to say that to someone who is depressed.

By its very nature, depression is elusive—hard to express or define. It's not just one single condition with one simple cause; it has all kinds of causes. As much as we understand the human brain compared to what we understood fifty years ago, we still have a long way to go. Sometimes something as wonderful as pregnancy can mess up brain chemistry so severely that you go home from the hospital with *two* things: a baby and postpartum depression. And that's a particularly tough one—because everyone, including you, figures you should be *thrilled* to have a baby . . . not seized with the wish to never see that baby again. Can you understand why that is so heartbreaking for a mother to experience? Can you please try to understand what that must feel like for her? Doing so will cause you to want to reach out to help instead of lash out in judgment.

And speaking of moms and babies, scientific evidence shows that you can *inherit* depression—or, at the very least, the tendency toward it—as part of your DNA. Serotonin, one of the neurotransmitters in your brain that also helps the neurons communicate (serotonin is associated with mood, sleep, appetite, and energy), is under "some genetic control," say the experts. Other tests show that the type of genetic matter you inherit—long or short—can make you either much more likely or much less likely to develop depression. (As a matter of fact, the same sorts of genetic material can predict the likelihood of things like suicide and other mental illnesses as well.)

In cases like this, one can't "control" depression any more than she can control blue eyes or long fingers. Can you imagine saying, "One thing I've learned is that eye color is a choice." You'd roll your blue eyes and laugh. Clearly, heredity is just one of many influences on depression, but it would be wise (and kind) to remember that many people truly are "born with it."

There are many kinds of treatment for depression. It takes a lot of experimenting to find out which one works.

Because depression has so many different causes, there are also all kinds of treatments for it. It can take a lot of experimenting to find which one works. Most often, it's a delicate combination of things that finally do the trick.

I'm pretty sure that you don't want anything too heavy, but let me give you just a little bit of background about what happens in depression. I promise it will be brief, and it will be simple. Depression occurs when the brain uses neurotransmitters faster than it can replace them. It can often show up after a time of sudden or prolonged stress. Without the right level of neurotransmitters, the neurons in the brain can't function like they're supposed to—they're not firing on all pistons—and that's something *completely* out of their control. Nobody can simply will a car to run without gasoline. The pleasure and reward centers in the brain stop working properly; in fact, sometimes they stop working completely. Even the stuff that used to make them happy feels bad. All that leads to the "perception error" of depression: to a depressed person, everything feels sad.

In the beginning stages, sleep patterns often become erratic.

Physical energy may start dropping off. The depression can cause you to lose your ability to concentrate. Your mind speed may increase and emotions can go off the charts. At this point, many people can simply take a break and their chemistry levels return to normal. Not so for someone with depression.

If untreated, a depressed person starts to find things that were once pleasant—a bowl of ice cream, a beautiful sunset, a giggling baby—as punishing instead of pleasing. Everything, even the good things, look grim. Let's imagine that someone compliments you on how great you look. A person who is not depressed takes it at face value and generally feels good as a result. A depressed person may feel bad and could think, *Why did she have to say that to me? Do I look needy or something? What does she want out of me, anyway?*

And here's the worst part: it's a vicious cycle. The stress—or anxiety—experienced by a depressed person further perpetuates the chemical problem in the brain. The stress depletes neurotransmitter levels further, making it even harder for the neurons to communicate normally, which intensifies the anxiety. The depression often produces the anxiety, and the anxiety fuels the depression. It is a cycle that can start to feel like a plane spiraling toward the ground.

> It's a vicious cycle. The depression produces the anxiety, and the anxiety fuels the depression. It starts to feel like a plane spiraling toward the ground.

If allowed to go further untreated, symptoms often get much worse. The mind starts torturing you. Your own brain seems to have turned against you. Some with depression describe the feeling of being possessed by someone else, someone who wants to hurt them. The mind starts to call up every bad experience and replays it over and over. Mind speed may increase even more, which means these thoughts feel inescapable because sleep may no longer give you respite. You may try to self-medicate with drugs or alcohol, anything to take away the torture. Fear and guilt become your constant companions. If still left untreated, suicidal thoughts start creeping into the mind. A depressed person doesn't see suicide as ending life—he or she sees it as an escape from the torture.

Sound awful? It is. And you don't have to look far to find someone who is battling exactly what I'm talking about: research shows that one out of every four people in this country has some form of depression, some to a greater extent than others. I'm not talking about having a bad day. I'm not talking about feeling down in the dumps after a favorite television show gets cancelled. I'm not talking about it raining on the day you visit Disneyland. I'm talking about a chemical problem in the brain that prevents neurons from working like they're supposed to. *One out of every four people experiences it.* That's an epidemic.

Research shows that one out of every four people in this country has some form of depression.

Let's put it this way. If you know three people, then—counting you—one of you is statistically likely to be depressed. Don't assume you know who in your life is struggling with depression. Human beings are good actors and actresses. Many with depression are able to fake their way through the day. A common phrase from friends and family after a suicide is, "I did not see it coming."

People in every walk of life suffer from depression. And don't think that fame exempts you. Check out just a few of the people from history who have battled debilitating depression. Abraham Lincoln, who referred to his depression as his "black dog," said, "I am now the most miserable man living." Authors Ernest Hemingway and Sylvia Plath both had severe depression, as did British Prime Minister Winston Churchill.

Former *60 Minutes* correspondent Mike Wallace, speaking at a White House conference on mental health, said of his depression, "I was lower than a snake's belly. And my own doctor, my own general practitioner, didn't pick it up. I used to call him in the middle of the night. And he said, 'Mike, you're strong. You'll get over it. You're strong.' Well, the fact of the matter is I didn't [get over it]."

For reasons that aren't completely understood, depression is twice as common among women. And it's not just adults; people of all ages suffer from depression. When it happens to kids and teenagers, it dramatically increases the likelihood of physical illness, drug abuse, tobacco use, and alcohol dependence when those kids grow up.

Depression has been called "the common cold" of mental illnesses—and, just like the common cold, it can have a variety of symptoms ranging from mild to severe. Remember: the part of the brain that exerts a lot of control isn't working like it should in depression, so a lot of physical symptoms tend to show up unannounced and unaccounted for. It's critical to remember that these physical symptoms are *not* imagined. They are real.

> **Depression is twice as common among women. And it's not just adults: people of all ages suffer from depression. It has been called "the common cold" of mental illnesses.**

Let me try to give you an idea of what it feels like to be depressed. I did a lot of research, read a lot of accounts, and studied everything I could. I found some intriguing stuff. Of all the things I studied, one account in particular really touched me; it was described in a TED Talk titled, "Depression, the Secret We Share." Here's how Andrew Solomon describes depression:

> I had always thought myself tough, one of the people who could survive if I'd been sent to a concentration

> camp. [But then] I found myself losing interest in almost everything. I didn't want to do any of the things I had previously wanted to do, and I didn't know why. The opposite of depression is not happiness, but vitality. And it was vitality that seemed to seep away from me in that moment. Everything there was to do seemed like too much work. I would come home and I would see the red light flashing on my answering machine, and instead of being thrilled to hear from my friends, I would think, *What a lot of people that is to call back*. Or I would decide I should have lunch, and then I would think, *but I'd have to get the food out and put it on a plate and cut it up and chew it and swallow it*, and it felt to me like [Jesus's] Cross.

You might think that people who feel like Solomon describes himself are—well, just not getting it. If so, think again. Solomon himself explained, "You know it's ridiculous. You know it's ridiculous while you're experiencing it. You know that most people manage to listen to their messages and eat lunch and organize themselves to take a shower and go out the front door and it's not a big deal, yet you are in its grip and you are unable to figure out any way around it."

Here's what it boils down to: You *know* your thoughts are out of whack, but you can't figure out how to step off the irrational merry-go-round and stand on solid ground again. You'd give anything to do so.

For Andrew Solomon, as happens with many people who have depression, he also developed anxiety—"like that feeling you have if you're walking and you slip or trip and the ground is rushing up at you." But instead of lasting half a second, it never stops. Talk about torment! Solomon says it's "a sensation of being afraid all the time but not even knowing what it is you're afraid of."

At that point in his depression, he says, Andrew Solomon started to think "it was just too painful to be alive," and the only reason he could think not to kill himself "was so as not to hurt other people."

Total torment.

Solomon's description tugged at my heart. You might really be feeling some empathy here as well. The way he described his

Anxiety is like the feeling you have when you trip and the ground is rushing up at you. But instead of lasting half a second, it never stops.

feelings really helped me understand depression. But here's the problem: since depression can have all kinds of causes, it can express itself in many different ways. Some people simply quit—they just give up. They decide that their present conditions, not to mention any possibilities of a future, are intolerable.

Those with severe depression seem to literally sink away from life. In this kind of situation, things seem to progress gradually. A person does less and less, abandons hobbies, loses interest in people, and simply gives up at work. For such a person, nothing brings pleasure; nothing feels good. Eventually, it seems there is no reason to go on. It can come all at once or it can come in waves or episodes. For some, the depression seems like a low-grade fever—not necessarily debilitating, but just enough to impact their lives for years on end.

Even the symptoms of depression can vary. Some depressed people can't sleep and suffer from poor appetite. Others sleep way too much, and during their waking hours they want to eat everything in sight. Many have accompanying anxiety; some do not.

For almost all people with severe depression, there is no pleasure in anything. Life simply flatlines. In his quest to make sense of his own depression, Solomon interviewed a bunch of people who eagerly volunteered that they too were depressed. One of the first people he interviewed described depression as "a slower way of being dead." Early on, says Solomon, "that was a good thing for me to hear because it reminded me that a slow way of being dead can lead to actual deadness." I know a woman whose husband suffered from severe depression. She described it as living with someone who was dead.

Depression is no laughing matter. It's serious business. As Solomon said, "It's the leading disability worldwide, and people die of it every day."

Solomon finally got on the road to healing when he woke up one morning and thought he'd had a stroke. He lay in his bed, completely frozen, totally unable to move. He remembers looking at the telephone and thinking, *Something is really wrong, and I should call for help*. But he couldn't. He couldn't do something as simple as move his arm, pick up the phone, and dial.

Depression is no laughing matter. It's serious business. It's the leading disability worldwide, and people die of it every day.

He stayed in that condition for an astonishing four full hours.

Finally, after four hours, the phone rang. Somehow, Solomon said, he managed to pick up the phone. "It was my father," he recalls, "and I said, 'I'm in serious trouble. We need to do something.'" The very next day he began a series of therapies that eventually led to the successful treatment of his depression.

I'm not going to discuss the various treatments for depression here; what works for one person may not work for another. In my experience, a treatment program that attacks the depression from all sides of life is the most effective. Think of it as a four-legged stool. You have to make sure you're doing things right physically (diet, exercise, screen time, and so on), medically (seeing a doctor, getting proper medication, and so on), emotionally (seeing a trained therapist, meditation, journal writing, and so on), and spiritually (praying, reading the scriptures, attending the temple, serving, and so on). Don't think focusing on just one of the legs will fix things. Make a plan to come at this problem from all four sides.

Above all, please know that treatment is available, and you don't have to continue to suffer in silence. Talk to someone. Talk to your parents. Open up to a trusted friend. Go and see your doctor. Solomon remembers a man who told him, "If I can just stick it out for another year, I think I can just get through this." Solomon's reply was as wise as the Solomon we know in the Bible: "You may get through it, but you'll never be thirty-seven again. Life is short, and that's a whole year you're talking about giving up. Think it through."

> You don't have to continue to suffer in silence. As Elder Holland advised, seek the advice of reputable people with certified training and professional skills.

Please just understand this: you don't have to do this on your own. You may not be capable of doing it on your own. Asking you to heal your own depression is asking you to fix a broken brain with a broken brain. The Lord has given us a plethora of resources and gifts. Let's take advantage of as many as possible. As Elder Holland said, "If things continue to be debilitating, seek the advice of reputable people with certified training, professional skills, and good values. Be honest with them about your history and your struggles. Prayerfully and responsibly consider the counsel they give and the solutions they prescribe. If you had appendicitis, God would expect you to seek a priesthood blessing *and* get the best medical care available. So too with emotional disorders. Our Father in Heaven expects us to use *all* of the marvelous gifts He has provided in this glorious dispensation."

Your physician may prescribe antidepressants—and if that happens, I hope you will give them a try. Make sure your physician understands what you are going through and how depression is affecting you personally. We have somehow created a culture in which the use of antidepressants is a badge of shame. No, no, no. You would never try to shame a cancer patient for using chemotherapy or a strep throat patient for taking an antibiotic. Yet too many people refer to antidepressants as "happy pills." These kind of sarcastic and derogatory terms can undermine a person's determination to get help. You have every right to be against the use of antidepressants, but it does not help your cause to demean those who use them and see a benefit from them. I personally believe that antidepressants, if used, should be one piece in a holistic program. Such a program would encourage someone to confront their depression through diet, exercise, proper sleep, therapy, medication, meditation, prayer, service, and any other thing that is beneficial.

Let me share an example of what this culture has done to people. I once heard of an expert who spoke on depression at a large medical convention where all kinds of diseases were being discussed. After his presentation, a woman—let's call her Patricia—managed to pull him aside and ask him some questions about the antidepressant medication she was taking.

> "Our Father in Heaven expects us to use *all* of the marvelous gifts He has provided in this glorious dispensation."

After he answered her questions, he asked her why she had not told her husband about her depression. Patricia said, "I can't tell my husband [let's call him James] about this. He just wouldn't understand. So I keep it from him." When the expert continued to encourage her to talk to James about her depression and the medication she was taking, she was adamant. "I'll try," she said, "but I really don't think he'd understand. He'd just tell me to make lemonade and get better."

Now get this: *two days later*, a man approached the same expert, wanting to talk about the medication he was taking. Lo and behold, it was James. Yup. Patricia's husband, in the flesh. After querying the good doctor about his medication, James said, "My wife just would not understand this. I just can't tell her."

Talk about a dangerous culture: Patricia and James were taking the same medication, trying to treat the same illness, in the same room, and hiding it from each other. What a tragedy. They were too ashamed or didn't trust that their spouse could really understand and accept that they had a problem outside of their control.

> **If you're trying to help someone else who is suffering while God is working His remedy, "the rest of us can help by being merciful, nonjudgmental, and kind."**

If you're trying to help someone else who is suffering, Elder Holland told us that while God is working His remedy, "the rest of us can help by being merciful, nonjudgmental, and kind."

Please, please—be gentle. If your son or brother or father has depression—just put your arm around him. Just listen. Let him explain if he wants to. Just let him lean on you if that's all he wants to do. You don't need to give advice. You don't need to fix it. Avoid prescribing action and advice before you understand. Just because something has worked for you does not mean it will work for them. That's like saying, "Oh, your eyes don't work well? Here—take my glasses! What? They don't work for you? Well, they help me! What's wrong with *you*?"

If you have to err, err on the side of gentleness.

If you're the one dealing with depression, Elder Holland reached out to you:

> Don't assume you can fix everything, but fix what you can. If those are only small victories, be grateful for them and be patient. Dozens of times in the scriptures, the

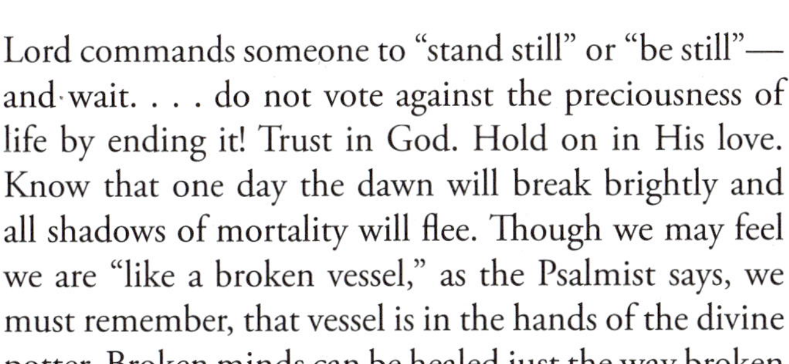

> Lord commands someone to "stand still" or "be still"—and wait. . . . do not vote against the preciousness of life by ending it! Trust in God. Hold on in His love. Know that one day the dawn will break brightly and all shadows of mortality will flee. Though we may feel we are "like a broken vessel," as the Psalmist says, we must remember, that vessel is in the hands of the divine potter. Broken minds can be healed just the way broken bones and broken hearts are healed.

I'm begging you not to suffer alone any longer. Talk to your spouse, or your parents, a close friend, a doctor, a church leader—talk to someone about it and get the help available. Then, when you are back on solid ground, you can help others.

CHAPTER SEVEN
Change

I HOPE YOU KNOW A lot more about happiness (and even depression) than when you started reading this book. If so, my work here is done—well, almost. How are you going to apply all you've learned here?

Here's a simple example of an important concept. The only piece of jewelry I wear is my wedding ring. Like most people, I wear it on the ring finger of my left hand. That's what I'm used to. That's where it belongs. Right?

> What if I put my wedding ring on my right hand instead of my left? It would drive me crazy. It would feel wrong. At least at first.

So what would happen if I took it off my left hand and put it on the ring finger of my right hand? It would drive me crazy. It would feel wrong. It would at the very least feel awkward—at least at first.

How long would it be before I no longer noticed that it was on my right hand? Maybe a few days. Maybe a few weeks. But after a certain period, I would naturally put that ring on my right hand without even thinking about it. Because now that's where it would belong. Right? It took a lot of energy at first, but now it's the norm.

There's a bit of science behind this. Let's say you decide you're going to make a change in your life. Guess how long it takes for you—the *whole* you—to accept that change? Most research says about fifteen days. At the fifteen-day mark, your mind and your heart and your emotions and all of the rest of you come to a stark realization: this change is going to be forever. Even those you live with begin to accept the change around the fifteen-day mark. This is how it is now. And we're okay with that.

When you try to make a change in your life, how long does it take the *whole* you to accept that change? Most research says about fifteen days.

Here's the problem: research also shows that when attempting to make a change, *most people give up after two weeks.* That's fourteen days—*one little measly day before you hit the jackpot.* One day shy of convincing your entire being that this change is permanent. That this is the new normal.

So choose the first thing you want to do and work on it until it becomes your new normal. Take at least fifteen days; three weeks or a month is even better. Focus your efforts on that one thing until you feel like you've gotten it right. The only way to make that change is to *practice*, and practice takes time and effort.

Here's a word of warning: your family or other loved ones will resist that change. Even if it's the best thing you've ever done for yourself (or them), they may dig in their heels and put up a fuss. Why? Because you've just threatened to shove them out of your comfort zone. And no one likes to be out of their comfort zone. I'm reminded of the time when, after listening to general conference, my parents decided we were going to read scriptures every day as a family. And even though we all knew this was a good thing, I don't think any of us made it too easy on my parents. I was fifteen, and my immediate thought was, *Oh, okay. I wonder how long* this *is going to last.*

I'll spare you the suspense. It lasted four days. Then we missed a day. But wait—the next day we were back at it again . . . for another two days. Then we missed a week. I think we did it one more day after that, but then the whole thing vaporized. We never reached that sweet spot of fifteen consecutive days. And we kids were not going to urge our folks on. Hey, it was outside our comfort zone. It wasn't our normal—not even close.

Back to you. If you're going to be making some changes so you can be happier, you're going to need some help. Lucky for you, I have a few strategies that have worked for me and that I've seen work for lots of other people.

First, make all of these positive changes a matter of prayer and fasting. Explain to the Lord how important these changes are to you and how you need His help. Search the Book of Mormon for any embedded message that will help you keep your drive alive.

Second, surround yourself with visual or tactile reminders. You might change your screensaver so you have a constant reminder of what you're trying to do. Maybe you can wear a new wristband; no one else will know what it means, but you will, and you'll be reminded of your goal every time you see it. Or maybe you can put something small in your pocket—such as a smooth pebble. Every time you touch it you'll get a gentle reminder (unless you're in the habit of carrying rocks around in your pocket). Before you know it, you'll see a change. And here's the amazing part: you will actually change the way your brain works. A happier brain means a happier you.

Another thing you should do is give yourself accountability. Before you give me *that look*, let me explain. Accountability is an incredible thing. It has a tremendous way of leading to success. And it's not all that hard. Best of all, it means you're not trying to do something that might be a bit challenging all on your own. You'll have help.

Here's what you do: Choose someone you love and trust. It needs to be someone who sees you a lot. If you suspect that your family might resist your efforts to change, then pick a good friend or coworker. Then put it all out there: Explain the change you're trying to make, and ask your trusted confidant to give you constant reminders. We're not talking nagging. We're talking an encouraging, how's-it-going, you-can-do-it, how-can-I-help sort of reminder.

Before you know it, you'll be reaching your goal. Then another. And another. You'll eventually be listening to uplifting music and taking a brisk walk every day and talking with your friends and getting a good night's sleep. As you recognize when you fall into the "future me" myth, you will decide to make changes today. You'll find yourself accentuating the positive and mindfully choosing your response to situations that used to push the edges of your patience. You'll be gentler with those with depression, and you'll get them to the experts who can help them.

And if this magic works the way it should, a wonderful thing will happen. You will be happier, and your friends and family will be happier too—just because you are around. Smiling, laughter, and peace will be the natural result of your presence.

Before you know it, a friend or family member is going to turn to you and say, "You are so happy. You are a light for me. I love being around you."

With a smile you'll say, "Thank you. That means a lot to me. I haven't always been this way, but I've been working hard on it."

They might respond with, "What have you been doing?"

Then, if you think they are emotionally ready, you might ask them, "Have I ever told you the story of the blue microwave?"

ABOUT THE AUTHOR

Hank Smith enjoys teaching in the Religious Education Department at BYU and is a favorite speaker for Especially for Youth, Best of Especially for Youth, and BYU Education Week.

Hank and his wife, Sara, were both born and raised in St. George, Utah. They are the parents of one daughter and four sons. Brother Smith enjoys running marathons and eating lots and lots of ice cream (which is why he runs marathons). More than anything else, he loves being at home spending all day with his wife and children.

You can follow him on Facebook at www.facebook.com/hanksmithcds